QUEER GOD DE AMOR

DISRUPTIVE CARTOGRAPHERS:
DOING THEOLOGY LATINAMENTE

Series editors: Carmen M. Nanko-Fernández,
Miguel H. Díaz, Gary Riebe-Estrella

This multivolume series re-maps theology and pushes out in new directions from varying coordinates across a spectrum of latinidad as lived in the USA. Authors reconfigure and disrupt key areas like revelation, pneumatology, eschatology, and Mariology. Other volumes complicate and advance even further key themes of significance in Latin@ theologies, including the option for culture, religious diversity, and the integral relationship between theologizing and praxis.

Previously published:

Miguel H. Díaz, editor, *The Word Became Culture* (Orbis)
Jean-Pierre Ruiz, *Revelation in the Vernacular* (Orbis)

Disruptive Cartographers: Doing Theology Latinamente

QUEER GOD DE AMOR

MIGUEL H. DÍAZ

Fordham University Press
New York   2022

Cover art: Jesus CIMI Alvarado, "Yolitzli," pastel on paper (2008).

Artist's description: "Yolitzli" is a self-portrait by Jesús "CIMI" Alvarado that envisions the artist within his complex Chicanx culture. CIMI finds inspiration in a Renaissance-era pose and in the image of the Sacred Heart. He pays homage to his birth-name and the influence that Catholicism had on his upbringing. Depicted on the left is a Mayan figure, who is adding three roses to his tattoo of the Sacred Heart. The three roses represent his mother and his two daughters. To CIMI's right is Mictlantecuhtli, the Aztec god of death that ruled the underworld.

Fordham University Press has no responsibility for the persistence or accuracy of URLs for external or third-party Internet websites referred to in this publication and does not guarantee that any content on such websites is, or will remain, accurate or appropriate.

Fordham University Press also publishes its books in a variety of electronic formats. Some content that appears in print may not be available in electronic books.

Visit us online at www.fordhampress.com.

Library of Congress Control Number: 2022913509

Printed in the United States of America
24 23 22   5 4 3 2 1
First edition

Por una extraña manera

mil vuelos pasé de un vuelo,

porque esperanza del cielo

tanto alcanza cuando espera;

esperé sólo este lance,

y en esperar no fui falto,

pues fui tan alto, tan alto,

que le di a la caza alcance.

—San Juan de la Cruz

A Michael,

carissimo compagno e amato da Dio

Contents

Preface to the Series

Disruptive Cartographers

Maps are functional and aesthetic. They establish and make visible place, space, time, and distance in terms of scale and relationships that are inevitably influenced by the cartographer's own coordinates. Mapping as a process is not as objective as it might seem, and the maps produced are not beyond bias. Maps are tools of power employed by empires to mark and represent their domains, territorially, economically, politically, culturally, religiously. Mapping also orients resistance by contesting borders, shifting perspective, challenging omissions, retrieving what was rendered invisible or insignificant, disrupting the illusion that certain maps or particular ways of mapping are necessarily normative.

Disruptive Cartographers is a multivolume series mapping theology from varying coordinates across a spectrum of latinidad as lived in the USA. Points of departure for Latin@ theologies are embedded in the complexities of la vida cotidiana, daily lived experience, which call forth a rich variety of responses from theologians who self-identify, in roots and commitments, as belonging to and emerging from the diversity found under such umbrella terms as Hispanic, Latino/a, Latinx, Latin@, Latin@. Explorations of lo cotidiano require a variety of lenses that must take into account intricate historical constructions that cannot easily shake off legacies of racism, sexism, heterosexism, classism, ableism, and colonialism. These legacies and their contemporary manifestations continue to influence sociopolitical contexts, theological formulations, and power and privilege differentials in church, academy, and society. The authors in this series have been left free to choose their own lenses and to probe those historical trajectories which most reflect their experience of the subject at hand. In this series in constructive theology some volumes seek to reconfigure such key areas as revelation, pneumatology, and eschatology, and others pursue themes significant in theologizing latinamente, including the option for culture, religious pluralism, and the relationship between theory and praxis. Each volume retrieves sources from within the historical stream of Latin@ theologies using contemporary experience as a guide. This series is not an introduction to Latino/a theology; it is not a comprehensive survey of contemporary Latinx theology; it is not an attempt to assert a monolithic or foundational Latin@ theology. Each volume offers a distinctive perspective on a topic familiar to systematic theologians. Accomplished latinamente, each reveals the complexity, diversity, and theological creativity that continues to emerge from within the community of Latino, Latina, Latinx theologians and scholars.

This distinctiveness is evident across the series volumes in a variety of ways. Within Latin@ theologies, socially locating one's perspective is an ethical obligation, an admission that our complicated identities and situated places from which we theologize form, inform, and reform our scholarship. Our fluid identities are expressed through a multiplicity of terms by which we name ourselves (Latino/a, Latinao, Latinoa, Latin@, Latin@, Latinx, Hispanic, Hispana, Hispano, Chican@, Tejana, Boricua, Cuban American are but a few). This self-naming is not a matter of semantics or political correctness but a claim that identity is a matter of theological anthropology. In this series there is no one imposed term, and each author provides their own rationale for their preferences. In addition, Latin@ theologies operate at the intersection of languages, and this hybridity may be reflected in the deployment of English, Spanish, and variations of Spanglish within texts. For Latinos/as Spanish is not a foreign language, and authors may choose not to italicize it in their respective volumes. Our preference for footnotes over endnotes reflects an understanding that they engage in a conversation literally on the same page as the body text. In this (at times) multilingual *conjunto* each maintains its integrity, and it is easier for readers to move from one to the other smoothly.

While each volume offers a distinctive and not a comprehensive perspective, authors situate themselves within the larger enterprise of doing theology latinamente and demonstrate that commitment by underscoring the relevance of lived experience as locus theologicus and by retrieving resources that draw from the depth and breadth of latinidad. Readers can begin their reading with any of the volumes in this series. Their commonality is to be found in the methods authors use to theologize; their diversity is in the historical sources and daily experience they privilege.

Ultimately, this series acknowledges that theological mapping matters for our communities of accountability too long left off or consigned to the margins of too many maps. At the same time, by allowing for creative and sustained development of constructive theological threads, familiar yet new, this series seeks to emulate the advice of Pope Francis to theologians: "Do not lose the ability for wonder; to practice theology in wonder."[1]

Carmen M. Nanko-Fernández,
Gary Riebe-Estrella, Miguel H. Díaz
Series Editors

---

[1] Pope Francis, "Audience with Members of the Italian Theological Association," December 29, 2017, http://press.vatican.va/content/sala-stampa/en/bollettino/pubblico/2017/12/29/171229c.html.

Acknowledgments

This book was conceived a couple of years ago in conversation with Dr. Carmen Nanko-Fernández, one of the co-editors of this series. As Carmen and I brainstormed possibilities for resourcing Latinx theologies, my decision to focus on Juan de la Cruz unfolded. Over the years, Carmen and I have become intellectual soulmates who have participated in numerous projects in service to the academy, the church, and society. I am grateful for her editorial suggestions during the writing of this project, which have helped me clarify and sharpen my theological arguments. Above all, I am grateful for her friendship and cannot thank her enough for her unconditional love and support during these past few years in my life.

I first became interested in trinitarian theology as a doctoral student at the University of Notre Dame. After taking Catherine M. LaCugna's course on the Trinity, I knew I wanted to pursue this subject for the rest of my life. From LaCugna, I learned that the doctrine of God is not an abstract reflection, but a doctrine that carries profound practical implications. LaCugna also had a great appreciation for Carmelite spirituality, especially the writings of John of the Cross. I am grateful that the seeds she planted before her passing away to God in 1997 have born much fruit throughout the years, especially in inspiring me to write this book on Juan's trinitarian theology of God.

As many of my close friends know, my coming out process has not been easy as a result of facing various familial, professional and ecclesial challenges. I am deeply grateful to the queer souls that I have met, especially the queer dads' support group at the Center on Halsted, a community center dedicated to advance and secure the health of queer persons. These men provided me much needed and life-saving support during my coming-out process. They have enriched my life with their stories of resilience and determination to survive and thrive while facing religious, familial, and social rejections. I am also grateful to Marianne Duddy-Burke, Executive Director of DignityUSA, and Francis DeBernardo, Executive Director of New Ways Ministry. Like so many, I too have benefited from their outstanding outreach and support for LGBTQ+ Catholics.

I am grateful to my colleagues in the Academy of Catholic Hispanic Theologians of the United States (ACHTUS). The work that we have undertaken *en conjunto* over the years, has drawn attention to marginalized persons and their often-forgotten human experiences. I see this book as part of the ongoing *projecto histórico* of Latinx theologians as we struggle to affirm the dignity and fundamental human rights of all human persons. In particular, I thank Jean Pierre Ruiz and Orlando O. Espín for the stimulating conversations that I have had with them while writing this book. These conversations led me to pursue various bibliographical sources that helped advance my central theological insights.

I also thank all my colleagues within and outside the Department of Theology at Loyola University Chicago. I am grateful for the conversations that I have had with Dr. Devorah Schoenfeld and Dr. Susana Cavallo. Schoenfeld is interested in medieval Bible commentaries and Jewish-Christian relations. Cavallo studies Spanish literary traditions, with a focus on gender and human sexuality. Their insights with respect to issues of gender, sexuality, and G*d in explicit religious texts and other literary traditions have provided invaluable leads for my research. I also express my gratitude to Zaccary Haney, my graduate assistant, for his help during the research, writing, and editing process. Finally, I am thankful to Loyola University of Chicago for my position as the John Courtney Murray, S.J., University Chair in Public Service. This chair supports much of my scholarship and my organization of and participation in scholarly conferences. In particular, I am grateful to Robert Divito, chair of the Theology Department, for his strong support of my various scholarly, teaching, and public engagements.

I am grateful to Michael Gibson, Robert Ellsberg, Maria Angelini, and, from Fordham University Press, John Garza, Richard Morrison, and Fredric Nachbaur for supporting my book and believing in the Disruptive Cartographers series. My gratitude extends to all who worked so hard to produce this volume. I thank the artist "CIMI" (Jesús Alvarado) for granting me permission to use his image "Yolitzli" for the cover of *Queer God de Amor*.

I thank Marian for her loving support during our twenty-three years of marriage, and mentoring me in the love of God, self-love, and loving others. I am grateful to our children Joshua, Ana, Emmanuel, and Miguel David. Their life-giving love over the years has meant the world to me. They are my pride and treasures, and I could not be happier and more honored to be their father. Finally, I am grateful to Michael. There are simply no words that could express my heart-felt gratitude for his extraordinary and God-like presence in my life and for his love, compassion, and understanding. He has accompanied me during very difficult times and has offered unwavering wisdom and support to the kids and to me. With one of his favorite lines from Juan's poems, I also state: "I hoped only for this way, and was right to wait for love, and climbed so high, high above, that at last, I caught my prey."[1]

---

[1] *The Poems of Saint John of the Cross*, trans. Willis Barnstone (New York: New Directions Books), 69.

A Note on References and Translations

References

All poems, commentaries, and letters cited from Juan de la Cruz in this book are taken from *San Juan de la Cruz: Obra completa,* vols. 1 and 2, ed. Luce López-Baralt and Eulogio Pacho (Madrid: Alianza Editorial, S.A., 2003).

All citations from John's poems are from *Obra completa,* vol. 1. The poems are cited in accordance with Spanish titles:

"Noche Oscura," or "Noche" abbreviated

"Cántico Espiritual"

"Llama de Amor Viva," or "Llama" abbreviated

The commentaries are cited in abbreviated form and according to Spanish titles:

S for *Subida del Monte Carmelo*

N for *Noche Oscura*

CE for *Cántico Espiritual*

Llama for *Llama de Amor Viva.*

Citations from commentaries of S and N come from *Obra completa*, vol. 1, and those of CE and Llama are from *Obra completa*, vol. 2.

For S and N, references are given according to book, chapter, and paragraph.

For CE, references are given according to stanza and paragraph.

For Llama, references are given according to stanza and paragraph.

Romances refers to the 9 theological poems that Juan de la Cruz wrote in 1578 on the Gospel text, *In principio erat Verbum* (John 1:1). Individual poems are referenced by number as they appear in *Obra completa*, vol. 1. These nine poems, sometimes referred to as ballads, are also accessible in English translations through various print and electronic sources.

Translations

Unless otherwise noted, translations and paraphrases from the Spanish are mine.

INTRODUCTION

Inflamed by God's Queer Love

En mi pecho florido que entero para él solo se
guardaba, allí quedó dormido,
y yo le regalaba, y el ventalle de cedros aire daba.[1]

This book is about the mystery of God and the relationship between divine and human persons. It explores this theology by turning to the teaching of Juan de la Cruz on mystical union with God and the analogue of sexual relationship that he uses to describe this union. Juan's mystical theology, which highlights the notion of God as lover and God's erotic-like relationship with human persons, provides a most fitting source to rethink the Christian doctrine of God. At the heart of trinitarian theology is the affirmation that God is personal and relational and that human persons created in God's image are also called to exist *from* and *for* others. As Catherine Mowry LaCugna points out, "Trinitarian theology could be described as par excellence a theology of relationship, which explores the mysteries of love, relationship, personhood and communion within the framework of God's self-revelation in the person of Christ and the activity of the Spirit."[2]

---

[1] "On my flowering chest that I saved for him alone, there he fell asleep as I caressed him, as the breezes from cedars fanned our bodies." In the poem "Noche Oscura," v. 6.

[2] Catherine M. LaCugna, *God for Us: The Trinity & Christian Life* (New York: HarperCollins, 1991), 1.

At the 1995 annual meeting of the Academy of Catholic Hispanic Theologians of the United States (ACHTUS) in New York, I raised the following question: "What would Catholic systematics look like if it were done latinamente?"[3] At that time, Orlando Espín and I coined the phrase "option for culture" to characterize the central methodological premise of Latinx theology.[4] Pursuant to this series' objective to draw from the depth and breadth of *latinidad* and to resource anew Latin@ theology, the question I raise now is as follows: What would the doctrine of God look like if it were done sanjuanistamente *and from the culture of the bedroom*?[5] As will become evident in the next five chapters, I embrace this sanjuanista reading of the doctrine of God as a way to "disrupt" the cartography of trinitarian theologies of God. In particular, I draw on Juan's analogy of sexual pursuit, seduction, and union to deepen and queer the mystery of God. This reinterpretation will invite the reader to reconsider God as the Queer God de Amor and the sexual union and relationships of queer persons as vestiges of the Trinity.

With the exception of Chapter 1, the other four chapters begin by citing a verse from Juan de la Cruz's poem "Living Flame of Love." Throughout the book, I have chosen to focus on the poem "Living Flame of Love" and on Juan's commentary on this poem, also titled *Living Flame of Love*, because of their rich mystical trinitarian theology.[6] In this poem, Juan uses courtship and sexual metaphors

---

[3] See Orlando O. Espín and Miguel H. Díaz, ed., *From the Heart of Our People: Latino/a Explorations in Catholic Systematic Theology* (Maryknoll, NY: Orbis Books, 1999), 1.

[4] Espín and Díaz, *From the Heart of Our People*, 3.

[5] The reader should note that the collective term used by scholars in reference to studies on Juan de la Cruz is "sanjuanista" studies. Please note I do not italicize this expression or its related terms throughout this book.

[6] On the rich doctrinal and more specifically trinitarian theology of these writings, see for instance, Colin P. Thompson, *St. John of the Cross:*

as analogues that describe the mystery of divine and human communion, a common approach in Spain in the sixteenth century. This theological approach offers a reading or gloss of literature *a lo divino*.[7] Unlike his poem *Cántico Espiritual*, which derives its inspiration *explicitly* from the Song of Songs, "Living Flame of Love" also relies on the peninsular Castilian tradition of popular and courtly love poems.[8] It is important to point out, however, that Juan writes "Living Flame of Love" and its commentary while he is also working on a second revision to his commentary on his poem "Spiritual Canticle" (1585–1586). This peninsular tradition has a long history of literature and interpretation that reflects the interdependence of religious and worldly realities. Indeed, Juan is heir to the rich cultural tradition of al-Andalus, as the Iberian Peninsula was known under Muslim rule from the eighth century to the fifteenth. During this time,

---

Songs in the Night (Washington, D.C.: Catholic University of America, 2003), 243–275. With respect to the poem, "Living Flame of Love," Colin Thompson observes how the very language and structure of the poem witnesses to the Triune mystery of God where the human experience of God always struggles to seek articulation (233, 256). With respect to the commentary, *Living Flame of Love*, he points out that "[i]t is also theologically the most searching, especially in its exploration of Trinitarian doctrine" (248).

[7] The expression *a lo divino* refers to a method Iberian writers used in the sixteenth century that took "secular" work and rewrote it with religious and theological overtones. In Llama (see note 4, *Obra completa*, vol. 2, 249, for historical note), Juan refers directly to Sebastián Córdoba's book *Las Obras de Boscán y Garcilaso trasladadas en materias cristianas y religiosas* (Granada, ES: 1575). See Sebastián Córdoba, *Garcilaso a lo divino: Introducción, textos y notas* (Ann Arbor: University of Michigan, 1971).

[8] See also Ian Macpherson, "Rompe la tela de este dulce encuentro: San Juan's 'Llama de amor viva' and the Courtly Context," in *Studies in Honor of Bruce W. Wardropper*, ed. Dian Fox, Harry Sieber, and Robert TerHorst (Newark, DE: Juan de la Cuesta, 1989), 195.

Christian, Muslim, and Jewish writers unabashedly addressed the subject of sexuality, including homoerotic love, and did so, in deeply religious terms. In his poem "Living Flame of Love" Juan reads human love, *a lo divino*, that is, in explicitly religious terms. In this sense, it is not so much the case that Juan takes the burning flame of sensual love "from its profane context into a spiritual context where it is refined into and redefined as the flame of the Holy Spirit."[9] Rather, in continuity with his Iberian roots, Juan fuses the two, and invites us to embrace the incarnational and thereby sacramental nature of daily living.

It is quite common for interpreters of Juan de la Cruz to separate the more theological from the more mundane aspects of his writings, and to spiritualize the latter. One of my fundamental arguments in this book is that this line of interpretation is alien to the cultural traditions that frame Juan's religious imagination. Shari Lowin points out, with respect to identifying literature of the time as secular, "The term and concept belong to the modern world-view."[10] In Muslim Spain, she writes, "rather than separating the spiritual world from the physical world, distinguishing between what the modern world deems the secular and the religious realms, these Muslim and Jewish authority figures fused the two."[11] Following this tradition, I seek to bridge rather than to separate mystical and sexual love and to resist the overwhelming tendency of Juan's interpreters to dismiss the profound theological significance of sexuality conveyed in Juan's writings. Thus, while

---

[9] Macpherson, "Rompe la tela de este dulce encuentro," 197. For a contemporary expression that relates religious and lived daily lived experiences, see Jean-Pierre Ruiz, "Beyond Borders and Boundaries: Rethinking Eisegesis and Rereading Ruth 1:16–17," in Miguel H. Díaz, *The Word Became Culture* (Maryknoll, NY: Orbis Books, 2021), 29–35.

[10] Shari L. Lowin, *Arabic and Hebrew Love Poems in Al-Andalus* (New York: Routledge Taylor & Francis Group), 22n2.

[11] Lowin, *Arabic and Hebrew Love Poems*, 1.

embracing the theological nature of his sexual metaphors, I part ways from those who characterize an erotic reading of his writings as an impoverishment of his theology.[12]

Juan composed the poem, "Living Flame of Love" in Granada (circa 1585). The first version of his commentary on this poem was also written around this time at the request of Doña Ana de Mercado y Peñalosa, "a wealthy lady living in Segovia who had come to know John of the Cross during a sojourn in Granada, and who had evidently received high mystical graces."[13] He redacted the commentary in La Pañuela in 1591.[14] In addition to focusing on this poem and its commentary, I also draw from his other poetry, especially his

---

[12] For instance, see Thompson, *St. John of the Cross: Songs in the Night*, 255. For an alternative line of interpretation in line with the approach taken in this book, see Willis Barnstone, *The Poetics of Ecstasy: Varieties of Ekstasis from Sappho to Borges* (New York: Holmes & Meier, 1983), 180–190; Daniel Muñoz, "The Spiritual Force of Unleashed Love: Echoes of Saint John of the Cross in Federico García Lorca's Sonnets of the Dark Love," *Spiritus; A Journal of Christian Spirituality* 18, no. 2 (2018): 152–175.

[13] George H. Tavard, *Poetry and Contemplation in St. John of the Cross* (Athens: Ohio University Press, 1988), 193. For a study of the two versions of the commentary, see *John of the Cross: The Living Flame of Love, Versions A and B*, ed. Jane Ackerman (Binghamton, NY: Medieval & Renaissance Texts & Studies, 1995). For an excellent discussion of the context and genre of Juan de la Cruz's poem and commentary (including his two redactions of the commentary), see Gabriel Castro, "Llama de Amor Viva," in *Introducción a la lectura de San Juan de la Cruz*, ed. Agustín García Simón (Salamanca, ES: Junta Castilla y León, 1991), 493–532. See also E. W. Trueman Dicken, *The Crucible of Love: A Study of the Mysticism of St. Teresa of Jesus and St. John of the Cross* (New York: Sheed and Ward, 1963), 464–465; Kieran Kavanaugh, "Introduction to Living Flames of Love," in *The Collected Works of John of the Cross*, trans. Kieran Kavanaugh and Otilio Rodriguez (Washington, DC: Institute of Carmelite Studies, 1991), 633–637.

[14] Bernard McGinn, *Mysticism in the Golden Age of Spain (1500–1650)*, vol. 6, part 2 of *The Presence of God: A History of Western Christian Mysticism* (New York: Crossroad, 2017), 242.

Romances (ballads). These nine poems, considered part of his "prison works," are recognized by scholars for their rich trinitarian content.[15] In them Juan reflects on the Prologue of John's Gospel to offer a window into God's life and the sharing of divine life that occurs as Christ unites with and becomes the spouse of humanity.[16]

Chapter 1 establishes my rationale for my choice of Juan de la Cruz's mystical theology and offers some arguments that anticipate the practical reasons for queering his theology. Chapter 2 disrupts God-talk by turning to the bedroom as a *locus theologicus*, examining issues related to knowing God in relationship to the senses and human sexuality. It names the triune mystery, underscoring Juan's apophatic understanding of God as "*un no sé qué*" ("an I know not what"). Chapter 3 focuses on the notion of God's self-communication, highlighting the intimate trinitarian indwelling in human persons that enables transformation, illumination, and union with God. Chapter 4 studies Juan's notion of divine and human persons as ecstatic, and thereby relational, beings. Chapter 5 concludes this sanjuanista resourcing of the doctrine of God by indicating some practical implications relative to Juan's mystical theology. It brings Juan's trinitarian theology into creative and critical conversation with queer theology, particularly the contributions of Latin American liberation theologian Marcella Althaus-Reid.[17]

---

[15] "The ballads on the Trinity provide a wider narrative and doctrinal framework for San Juan's whole poetic enterprise, and link the passionate and sensuous encounter of the two lovers in the liras with the divine Trinity's embrace of all humanity through use of the same fundamental image, the marriage." See Thompson, *St. John of the Cross: Songs in the Night*, 55. See also McGinn, *Mysticism in Golden Age of Spain*, 241, 245–35. On Juan's poetry, see also Tavard, *Poetry and Contemplation*, esp. 37–51, 53–73, 117–136, 181–246.

[16] See *Romances*, 3.

[17] For instance, Marcella Althaus-Reid, *The Queer God* (New York:

Relating Juan's mystical trinitarian theology to the daily lived experiences of human sexuality and the sexual subject offers new resources and insights into Christian theological traditions, and to theologies done latinamente. Theology done sanjuanistamente: (1) bridges the Christian spirituality of a Spanish mystic and the doctrine of God in relationship to the experience of human sexuality; (2) challenges some existing interpretations of Juan's mystical theology, drawing on his works in Spanish rather than relying on English-language translations, in order to highlight the incarnational nature of his trinitarian theology; (3) expands conventional interpretations of his mystical theology, which tend to minimize his sexual analogies and interpret them through a heteronormative lens; and (4) queers Juan's notions of divine and human persons as a way to deepen the Catholic analogical imagination. In Juan, we can discover that theological "queerness" is "not entirely alien to the theological tradition,"[18] but in fact, is essential to affirm the mystery of God.

Mapping the Christian doctrine of God sanjuanistamente and queering this theology, questions and contests established theological borders, shifts perspectives, challenges omissions, and

---

Routledge, 2003); idem, "Queer I Stand: Lifting the Skirts of God," in *The Sexual Theologian*, ed. Marcella Althaus-Reid and Lisa Isherwood (New York: T & T Clark, 2004), 99–109; Linn Marie Tonstad, *God and Difference: The Trinity, Sexuality, and the Transformation of Finitude* (New York: Routledge, 2016); Sarah Coakley, *God, Sexuality, and the Self* (Cambridge, UK: Cambridge University Press, 2013); Rolf R. Nolasco Jr., *God's Beloved Queer: Identity, Spirituality and Practice* (Eugene, OR: Wipf & Stock, 2019); Susannah Cornwall, "Stranger in Our Midst: The Becoming of the Queer God in the Theology of Marcella Althaus-Reid," in *Dancing Theology in Fetish Boots,* ed. Lisa Isherwood and Mark D. Jordan (London: SCM Press, 2010), 95–112; Gavin D'Costa, "Queer Trinity," in *Queer Theology: Rethinking the Western Body*, ed. Gerard Loughlin (Malden, MA: Blackwell, 2007), 269–280.

[18] See Cornwall, "Stranger in Our Midst," 103. Here, she argues that Althaus-Reid at times has not sufficiently recognized how her queer theology is not entirely alien to the theological tradition.

retrieves what has been rendered theologically invisible or insignificant. Parting from interpretations that sanitize and spiritualize Juan's mystical theology, and thereby undermine the manifold ways that he affirms an embodied relationship with God, I argue that his theology is necessarily, as any Christian theology should be, firmly rooted in an incarnational spirituality. In this sense, his theology is not anti-body, as some might be prone to suggest given its radical apophatic nature. Instead, what his theology affirms is a theocentric perspective that sets God free from idolatrous constructions, and having been set free, enables us to encounter the divine in diverse persons and human experiences.

In order to unite and be transformed in God, Juan invites us to embrace active and passive dark nights related to our spiritual faculties and bodily senses. These nights reorient human persons to God.[19] In turn, this human orientation to God creates the possibility for an embodied way of knowing, that is, savoring (from the Spanish verb *saber*) God and all human experiences in God, including sexuality. This sanjuanista epistemology echoes Ignacio Ellacuría's observation that it is not so much the case that "God is in all things," but rather, that "all things, each in its own way, have been grafted with the triune life and refer essentially to that life."[20]

All theology is contextual, and to some degree all theology is also autobiographical. It reflects the cartographies of theologians, their daily life experiences, their dark nights, and their moments of theological illuminations. In the spirit of Latinx and queer theologies, which seek disclosure with respect to the contexts that inform

---

[19] See Ruth Burrows, *Ascent to Love: The Spiritual Teaching of St. John of the Cross* (Denville, NJ: Dimension Books, 1987).

[20] Ignacio Ellacuría, cited in Miguel H. Díaz, "The Life-Giving Reality of God from Black, Latin American, and US Hispanic Theological Perspectives," in *The Cambridge Companion to the Trinity*, ed. Peter C. Phan (New York: Cambridge University Press, 2011), 259.

theological endeavors, I want to state the following: As a Cuban American, as a queer man, and as Catholic, this book speaks to my own personal and communal *lucha*—the challenge in reconciling my cultural and sexual struggles, as well as my individual and communal experiences, and my private and public life. Common to Latinx and queer theologies is an understanding of theology "as a first person theology: diasporic, self-disclosing, autobiographical and responsible for its own words."[21]

This book was birthed from this personal struggle and from the experience of standing in solidarity with the struggles of numerous queer persons whom I have been privileged to meet and accompany since I started the process of coming out to myself, family, and friends. Coming out is not always as liberating as it is oftentimes assumed to be, as anyone who has accompanied LGBTQ+ persons (in particular, brown and black queer bodies) knows. Cultural realities connected to my Cuban background and to my Catholic faith obstructed my journey of self-discovery and self-transparency. As is the case for many queer persons, coming out involves an ongoing wrestling with angels to reject powers and principalities that stand in the way of human flourishing and our ability to know and unite with God and neighbor.[22] Shame-based trauma, often related to ill-conceived religious ideas, theologies, and religious practices, keeps many of us from beginning and continuing this process.[23]

---

[21] Althaus-Reid, *The Queer God* (New York: Routledge, 2003), 8.

[22] See Brian Bouldrey, ed., *Wrestling with the Angel: Faith and Religion in the Lives of Gay Men* (New York: Riverhead Books, 1995).

[23] On a classic study on shame-based trauma, see Alan Downs, *The Velvet Rage: Overcoming the Pain of Growing up Gay in a Straight Man's World* (Philadelphia: Da Capo Press, 2005). See also Gershen Kaufman and Lev Raphael, *Coming Out of Shame: Transforming Gay and Lesbian Lives* (New York: Doubleday, 1996); Jeff Chu, *Does Jesus Love Me: A Gay Christian's Pilgrimage in Search of God in America* (New York: HarperCollins, 2013); Bouldrey, *Wrestling with the Angel: Faith and Religion in the Lives of Gay Men.*

Confronting and accepting one's queer humanity in the midst of strong opposition from familial, cultural, and religious influences can be quite daunting and for some life-threatening. Doing so, at the risk of losing life-sustaining commitments and communal relationships, makes the coming-out process even more difficult. But this is the story of many men like myself and the queer men whom I have been privileged to accompany. Their stories speak to the resilience of the human spirit not to simply accept life as is, but to change and transform life. "*Yo viviré y sobreviviré,*" Celia Cruz sings in her rendition of Gloria Gaynor's 1978 anthem of survival, a defiant affirmation of existence in the face of pain and marginalization.[24]

This book represents an exercise in critical reflection on the Christian praxis of sexuality.[25] It joins other contemporary theological efforts that have challenged Christian theologies of God from feminist and queer perspectives.[26] It outs God from heteronorma-

---

[24] See Celia Cruz, "Yo Viviré—I Will Survive," on the album *Siempre Viviré* (*Sony Music, 2000*). On the significance and power of Gloria Gaynor's song "I Will Survive," see Karen Grigsby Bates, "'I Will Survive Saves Marginalized People a Spot on the Dance Floor," *All Things Considered*, National Public Radio, September 24, 2019, https://www.npr.org/2019/09/24/763518201/gloria-gaynor-i-will-survive-american-anthem.

[25] The definition builds on Gustavo Gutiérrez's famous definition of liberation theology as "a critical reflection upon Christian praxis in light of the word of God." See *A Theology of Liberation* (Maryknoll, NY: Orbis Books, 1988), xxix.

[26] For instance, see Elizabeth Johnson, *She Who Is: The Mystery of God in Feminist Theological Discourse* (New York: Crossroad, 1992); Rosemary Radford Ruether, *Sexism and God-Talk: Toward a Feminist Theology* (Boston, MA: Beacon Press, 1983); and Gail Ranshaw, *God beyond Gender* (Minneapolis: Fortress Press, 1995); Althaus-Reid, *The Queer God*; Gavin D'Costa, *Sexing the Trinity: Gender, Culture and the Divine* (London: SCM Press, 2000).

tive closets, and outs human sexuality to resource theology. This outing of the queerness of divine and human life will enable us to better align theoretical reflections on the mystery of God with the faith experiences of queer Catholics.[27] I turn to Juan as a mystical disruptor within the Christian tradition, as an ally that can help us rethink theologically the experience of sexuality and the sexual subject in ways more liberating to queer Christians.

As queer Catholics, we share Juan de la Cruz's deep desire to enter into an intimate relationship with God, and like Juan, we are seduced into this relationship by the breath of the Spirit, God's living flame of love. Divine seductions are consummated when persons, regardless of their sexual orientations and gender identities, set aside all that stands in the way of God and enter the divine chambers ready to fall asleep with, caress, and unite with Christ, their beloved spouse. Juan teaches us that in union with Christ, persons come to "know" God, all that is not God, and all things in God.

---

[27] Althaus-Reid argues, "Queer Theology is a process of Outing Theology as a method for action and reflection, in the sense that first of all, Classical theology needs to come clean with its real sexual identity, from where goals and objectives can be worked out." See Marcella Althaus-Reid, "Outing Theology: Thinking Christianity out of the Church Closet," *Feminist Theology* 9, no. 27 (2001): 60.

1

Doing Theology Sanjuanistamente

Y así espero que, aunque se escriban aquí algunos
puntos de teología escolástica acerca del trato
interior del alma con su Dios, no será en vano
haber hablado algo a lo puro del espíritu en tal
manera; pues, aunque a Vuestra Reverencia le
falte el ejercio de teología escolástica con que se
entienden las verdades divinas, no le falta el de
la mística, que se sabe por amor, en que no sola-
mente se saben, mas justamente se gustan.[1]

To do theology sanjuanistamente is to be seduced by divine
love. For Juan de la Cruz mysticism provides a way of knowing
God via a love in which one not only knows but also savors the
beloved, "*no solamente se saben, mas justamente se gustan.*"[2] This

---

[1] "And I hope that although I will write about some scholastic theological principles concerning the subject of the soul's intimacy with God,
even though your Reverence lacks training in scholastic theology through
which one understands divine truth, you do not lack mystical understanding through which one knows by the way of love, in which one not
only knows but also savors." In Prologue, CE, 3.

[2] Juan addresses these words to a Carmelite nun named Ana de Jesús
for whom he writes the commentary to his poem, "The Spiritual Canticle."
Chapter 2 explores in more detail the epistemological significance of this
way of knowing via a way of a love that savors God.

1

mystical way of relating to God flows through the rhythms and words of his sixteenth-century Spanish poetry and commentaries. In keeping with the premise of this series to disrupt and rethink Christian theology *latinamente*, I initiate my methodological discussion en lo cotidiano, in daily living, and in particular, in human experiences that shaped Juan's mystical theology as well as those that have shaped Latinx theologies.[3] A brief biographical sketch helps contextualize Juan's writings because, as Thomas F. O'Meara observes, "The first step in understanding great human creations is to set them aside for a while and learn about the age and the person who produced them."[4] This retrieval of Juan's mystical theology offers an Iberian source that is helpful, yet often overlooked, in trinitarian theology.[5] The richness of his mystical theological language, and the intimacy it suggests through sexual imagery, reminds us of our intrinsic theocentric orientation, that is, of our "capacity for relationship, for ecstasis, and for self-transcendence."[6] Finally, I entertain the "queering" of Juan's theology as a fitting option for exploring the practical and sexual implications of his trinitarian theology.[7]

---

[3] A note on nomenclature: Throughout the book I use terms such as U.S. Hispanic, Latin@, Latino/a, Latin@, Latinx, interchangeably as a way to represent the diverse communal forms of identification associated with these communities. The term "queer" and its theological connections is explored in greater depth in Chapter 5.

[4] Thomas F. O'Meara, *Thomas Aquinas: Theologian* (Notre Dame, IN: University of Notre Dame Press, 1997), 1.

[5] Some contemporary trinitarian contributions include: Walter Kasper, *The God of Jesus Christ* (New York: Crossroad, 1989); Peter Phan, ed. *The Cambridge Companion to the Trinity* (Cambridge: Cambridge University Press, 2011); Catherine M. LaCugna, *God for Us: The Trinity & Christian Life* (New York: HarperCollins, 1991); Elizabeth A. Johnson, *She Who Is: The Mystery of God in Feminist Theological Discourse* (New York: Crossroad, 1992).

[6] LaCugna, *God for Us*, 407.

[7] On understanding what theologians mean when they use the noun

Juan de la Cruz, a Disruptive Theological Voice

Juan de Yepes y Álvarez was born in the little Castilian town of Fontiveros in 1542.[8] His mother, Catalina, was a poor weaver, likely of Moorish background, and his father, Gonzalo, was from a family of *conversos*, descendants of Jewish converts to Catholicism.[9] Spain at this time was under the rule of Charles V and was preoccupied with issues of cultural and religious purity. Juan grew up in a hybrid culture that reflected Christian, Jewish, and Muslim interactions. His writings reflect this cultural and religious hybridity.[10]

As a youth, Juan ministered to sick persons in a local hospital. He received a Jesuit education, but at the age of twenty-one in 1563, instead of joining the Jesuits, he decided to enter the Carmelite order at a house that had been established in Medina. As is customary for men and women to do when they enter religious communities, he took a new name, the name of Juan de San Mátias. The Carmelites later sent him off for three years to study philos-

---

or adjective "queer" or the verb "to queer," see Chris Greenough, *Queer Theologies: The Basics* (New York: Routledge, 2020), 4, 1–62; Meg-Juan Barker and Julia Scheele, *Queer: A Graphic History* (London: Allen & Unwin, 2016); Linn Marie Tonstad, *Queer Theology* (Eugene, OR: Cascade Books, 2018), 1–15.

   [8] For these biographical details, I rely on Bernard McGinn, *Mysticism in the Golden Age of Spain (1500–1650)*, vol. 6, part 2, of *The Presence of God: A History of Western Christian Mysticism* (New York: Crossroad, 2017).

   [9] See McGinn, *Mysticism in the Golden Age of Spain*, 231–238. For a more detailed account of his life see, Antolín Fortunato, *Primeras biografías y apologías de San Juan de La Cruz* (Salamanca, ES: Junta de Castilla y León, 1991); Luis Antonio Vega, *San Juan de la Cruz: Su vida, Sus mejores páginas, Su época* (Madrid: Nuevas Editoriales Unidas, 1961).

   [10] On the sources and resources of Juan's writings, see McGinn, *Mysticism in the Golden Age of Spain*, 242–245; Willis Barnstone, *The Poetics of Ecstasy: Varieties of Ekstasis from Sappho to Borges* (New York: Holmes & Meier, 1983), 163–172.

ophy and theology at the University of Salamanca. And in 1567, when Juan was ordained a priest, he met Teresa of Ávila who had begun reforming the Carmelite order.[11] Teresa convinced Juan to join the reforms of the Carmelite order. He agreed and changed his name to Juan de la Cruz. He became her companion and spiritual director, a partner in reformation who endured opposition from members of the Carmelite order.

Juan suffered many trials and tribulations. "He learned about deprivation and marginalization from the very start of his life in Spain in 1542."[12] These experiences, however, rather than deter his creativity, in fact propelled him to write. In 1576, Juan was briefly arrested by members of the unreformed Carmelite order, also known as Observants. The next year the Observants abducted him in Ávila and imprisoned him in a small cell in Toledo. It was during these nine months of confinement that Juan began to write the poems that became the foundational source of his mystical theology.[13] His poems have been described as "quasi-scriptural texts" that internalize the world of Scripture into his own experi-

---

[11] On Teresa of Ávila, see Teresa de Ávila, *The Life of Saint Teresa of Ávila by Herself,* trans. J. M. Cohen (London: Penguin Books, 1957); Teresa of Ávila, *The Collected Works of St. Teresa of Ávila,* trans. Kieran Kavanaugh, O.C.D., and Otilio Rodriguez, O.C.D. (Washington, DC: Institute of Carmelite Studies, 1976); McGinn, *Mysticism in the Golden Age of Spain,* 120–229.

[12] Richard P. Hardy, "Liberated to Become God: The Mystical Path of St. John of the Cross," *Grail,* vol. 10, no. 1/2 (1994): 130. Note also the following personal account of his suffering: "I often heard him speak of the persecutions and trials which he had suffered at the beginning of his career and of how the calced Fathers had kept him in prison for nine months, giving him the discipline every Friday, and, as food, bread and water. I can testify that his shoulders were so sore that on one day he could not bear the serge of his habit and I believe he told me that it was due to this." See "Account of the Life of the Saint by Fray Juan Evangelista, Prior of Caravaca," in *The Complete Works of Saint John of the Cross,* trans. Silverio de Santa Teresa, C.D. (Westminster, MD: Newman Bookshop, 1946), 360.

[13] See McGinn, *Mysticism in the Golden Age of Spain,* 232–236.

ence.[14] They represent Juan's attempt "to inhabit the scripture more deeply," paralleling his attempt "to enter into the interior relationship with God as far as is possible."[15]

Three of the poems he wrote, "The Dark Night," "The Spiritual Canticle," and "Living Flame of Love," became the source that inspired his four major prose commentaries, *The Ascent of Mount Carmel*, *The Spiritual Canticle*, *The Dark Night*, and *Living Flame of Love*.[16] He wrote "Living Flame of Love" and his commentary on the poem toward the end of his life (1584–1585).[17] Although his other poems and commentaries touch on the subject of God's trinitarian life, the focus of this poem and commentary is itself God's trinitarian life in the soul. In these last major writings, as he had done in his other poems and commentaries, he taps into human sexuality and the sexual subject, and interprets these experiences *a lo divino*.

On December 13, 1591, Juan surrendered his life to this triune mystery. He passed away at midnight, joining his beloved spouse, consummating a relationship between human and divine consumed throughout his life in the Holy Spirit, God's living flame of love.[18] On this happy night, when God liberated Juan from all earthly

---

[14] Edward Howells, *John of the Cross and Teresa of Avila: Mystical Knowing and Selfhood* (New York: Crossroad, 2002), 18.

[15] Howells, *John of the Cross and Teresa of Avila*, 18.

[16] For historical context and a summary of content of these commentaries, see McGinn, *Mysticism in the Golden Age of Spain*, 267–313. Beyond poems and commentaries attributed to Juan are maxims, sayings, letters, and *Avisos y Cautelas*, a series of short spiritual counsels and precautions written for the Carmelites. See *Obra completa*, vol. 2, 355–427.

[17] See Gabriel Castro, "Llama de Amor Viva," in *Introducción a la lectura de San Juan de la Cruz*, ed. Agustín García Simón (Salamanca, ES: Junta de Castilla y León, 1991), 493–532.

[18] In his writings Juan speaks of divine love as both consuming and consummating. See CE, 39, 14, where he connects "flame" to the Holy Spirit and speaks of this flame as consummating and consuming. This line in CE is important because it foreshadows the subject of his last major poem, "Living Flame of Love," and his commentary on this poem.

tribulations, he becomes a living poem. This was the night he often imagined when he wrote about God turning darkness into the dawn of day. Here he most radically embodied "The Dark Night."[19]

> *¡Oh noche, que guiaste!*
> *¡Oh noche amable más que el alborada!*
> *¡Oh noche que juntaste*
> *Amado con amada,*
> *amada en el Amado transformada.*[20]

With these words Juan highlights the climax of the union between "lover and beloved, transforming one into the other." Sexual union becomes a human analogue of the mystical joining of divine and human persons.

A Starting Point in Ordinary and Daily Living

"A genuine Christian who lives the mysticism of daily life possesses the bold, but often hidden, confidence that ordinary daily life is the stuff of authentic life and real Christianity."[21] Among the salient features of Latinx theology is critical engagement with daily living or what Latin@ theologians characterize as lo cotidiano. As Carmen Nanko-Fernández proposes, "For any number of Latin@ theologians lo cotidiano functions as locus theologicus . . . that provides content, particularizes context, and marks the spaces and

---

[19] Carta, "A Catalina de Jesús, Carmelita Descalza," in *Obra completa*, vol. 2, 391–92. The poem was composed shortly after his escape from his imprisonment, a confinement that he describes as a time when he resided in the "belly of the whale" (Jonah 2:1–2).

[20] "O night that guided! O night more friendly than the dawn! O night that joined, lover and beloved, transforming one into the other." In poem "Dark Night," v. 5.

[21] See Harvey D. Egan, *Karl Rahner, Mystic of Everyday Life* (New York: Crossroad, 1998), 59.

place(s) from which Latin@s *do* theology."[22] In this book, Juan's mystical theology provides content to help understand the mystery of God. His mystical theology also particularizes context, mainly by inviting us to consider, *a lo divino*, ordinary human experiences associated with sexuality, the sexual subject, and cultures of the bedroom. Above all, his mystical theology relocates theology from "desktops" to ordinary places where we encounter God's transformative triune life at work in the lives of real persons.[23] "For several decades" observes Shawn Copeland, "theologians have bemoaned theology's break or estrangement from spirituality, from mysticism. Healing this rupture begins where theology exists—the minds and hearts and prayer and lives of theologians."[24] In this case, my theology begins with Juan's mind, heart, prayer, and love story and his attentiveness to human sexual relations as vestiges of divine life.

Mysticism and Sexuality

Latin@ theologies have engaged issues of gender, drawing on women's experiences to construct, understand, and name, in various ways, the mystery of God.[25] The same cannot be said with

---

[22] Carmen M. Nanko-Fernández, "Lo Cotidiano as Locus Theologicus," in *The Wiley Blackwell Companion to Latino/a Theology*, ed. Orlando O. Espín (Oxford: Wiley-Blackwell, 2015), 15.

[23] See Pope Francis, "Letter of his Holiness Pope Francis to the Grand Chancellor of the 'Pontificia Universidad Católica Argentina' for the 100th Anniversary of the Founding of the Faculty of Theology," March 3, 2015, http://www.vatican.va/content/francesco/en/letters/2015/documents/papa-francesco_20150303_lettera-universita-cattolica-argentina.html.

[24] Shawn Copeland, *Desire, Darkness, and Hope: Theology in a Time of Impasse* (Collegeville, MN: Liturgical Press, 2021), 50.

[25] For instance, see Jeanette Rodríguez, "God Is Always Pregnant," in *The Divine Mosaic: Women's Images of the Sacred Other*, ed. Theresa King (St. Paul, MN: International Publishers, 1994), 112–126; Ada María Isasi-Díaz, *La Lucha Continues* (Maryknoll, NY: Orbis Books, 2004), 24–34; Orlando O. Espín, "An Exploration into the Theology of Grace and Sin,"

respect to addressing the experience of human sexuality and the sexual subject.[26] I propose that Juan's writings provide a source to grapple with this lacuna and broaden the experiential horizon that informs our theologies.

Sexuality and particular sexual subjects per se are not the focus of Juan's mystical theology. His focus is undoubtedly on the love journey that leads the human person to union with God. Still, the analogies Juan draws to explore this relationship and mystery of divine love draw heavily from the experience of human sexuality. In comparing divine and human life and offering rich metaphors that trigger the sexual imagination, Juan reflects the Catholic analogical imagination. Coined by David Tracy, analogical imagination affirms the ability of human experiences to express a similarity-in-difference between divine and human life.[27] In this sense, Juan's theology of mystical union, especially as described in "Living Flame of Love," and in his commentary on this poem, enables us to return the erotic to the heart of trinitarian theology. As Mark D. Jordan opines,

---

in *From the Heart of Our People* (Maryknoll, NY: Orbis Books, 1999), 121–152; Ada María Isasi-Díaz, *En la Lucha, In the Struggle: A Hispanic Women's Liberation Theology* (Minneapolis: Fortress Press, 1993); Maria Pilar Aquino, Daisy Machado, and Jeanette Rodriguez, eds., *A Reader in Latina Feminist Theology: Religion and Justice* (Austin, TX: Austin University Press, 2002); Michelle A. Gonzalez, *Created in God's Image: An Introduction to Feminist Theological Anthropology* (Maryknoll, NY: Orbis Books, 2007); Nancy Pineda Madrid, *Suffering and Salvation in Ciudad Juárez* (Minneapolis: Fortress Press, 2011); Loida I. Martell-Otero, Zaida Maldonado Pérez, Elizabeth Conde-Frazier, *Latina Evangelicas: A Theological Survey from the Margins* (Eugene, OR: Cascade Books, 2013).

[26] See James B. Nickoloff, "Sexuality: A Queer Omission in US Latino/a Theology," *Journal of Hispanic/Latino Theology* 10, no. 3 (2003): 31–51.

[27] On the Catholic analogical imagination, see David Tracy's classic study *The Analogical Imagination: Christian Theology and the Culture of Pluralism* (New York: Crossroad, 1998).

Official saints are presumed to have acquired sexual purity early on in their journeys toward God. Indeed, we have heard from some spiritual authors that the absence of even involuntary arousal is an index of one's spiritual progress. But then, meeting God, the mystics are overwhelmed with what is in some cases marked by the physiological effects of sexual intercourse and described in all cases with the imagery of that intercourse. Mystical experience seems not so much an allegory of the erotic as its return.[28]

By tapping into human sexuality to inform his trinitarian theology, Juan opens the door for understanding not only the erotic elements of mystical experiences but also the mystical elements in erotic experiences. In this sense, this classical yet disruptive voice connected to our cultural roots as Latinx theologians, recovers sexuality and the sexual subject as an essential source to think theologically. Connecting mysticism and sexuality, this sanjuanista reading of an ordinary human experience connected with daily living also prompts consideration of the religious and popular significance of sexuality and the bedroom.

Mysticism and Popular Catholicism

Religion, sexuality, and the bedroom are not absent from the Iberian sources that have influenced Latinx theologies. Stories of the Virgin Mary inserting herself between a bride and bridegroom to disrupt sexual intercourse or of the Spanish Inquisition charging Christians for their sexual, and in particular homoerotic, imaginations suffice to

---

[28] Mark D. Jordan, *The Ethics of Sex* (Malden, MA: Blackwell, 2001), 165. See also Michael Bernard Kelly, *Christian Mysticism's Queer Flame: Spirituality in the Lives of Contemporary Gay Men* (New York: Routledge Taylor & Francis Group, 2019).

make this point.[29] Juan's mystical theology not only returns the erotic to theology but also provides a way to expand our understandings of popular and religious experiences.

Latinx theologians have used the term "popular Catholicism" in connection with the religious experiences, symbols, and devotions of faith associated with "the people," especially marginalized persons and communities.[30] Reflections on this subject often revolve around religious practices within the familial spaces of the home. Retrieving and resourcing Latin@ theologies of God sanjuanistamente reinterprets the "popular" and "religious" elements of daily life, and relocates to the bedroom, the domestic presence of God typically associated with the popular devotion of "home altars."[31] In Latinx theology, the home altar is a symbol of God's intimate and personal presence, "a sort of theophanic manifestation of the divine presence in one's home."[32] In Juan's theology, the body, and more specifically, the union of sexual bodies, serves as a

---

[29] See Carmen Nanko-Fernández, "Playing en Los Márgenes: Lo Popular as *Locus Theologicus*," in *The Word Became Culture*, ed. Miguel H. Díaz, Disruptive Cartographers: Doing Theology Latinamente (Maryknoll, NY: Orbis Books, 2021), 93–113, and Jacqueline Holler, "'More Sins than the Queen of England': Marina de San Miguel before the Mexican Inquisition," in *Women in the Inquisition: Spain and the New World,* ed. Mary E. Giles (Baltimore: Johns Hopkins University Press, 1999), 209–28.

[30] For a discussion on the notion of what Latin@ theologians consider "popular," see Miguel H. Díaz, *On Being Human: U.S. Hispanic and Rahnerian Perspectives,* (Maryknoll, NY: Orbis Books, 2001), 62–63. In Latin@ theologies the "popular" often refers to persons and places related to marginalization and vanquishment. See the various reflections by Orlando O. Espín, especially, "Popular Religion as an Epistemology (of Suffering)," *Journal of Hispanic/Latino Theology* 2, no. 2 (1994): 66; and *The Faith of the People: Theological Reflections on Popular Catholicism* (Maryknoll, NY: Orbis Books, 1997), esp., 156–179.

[31] See C. Gilbert Romero, *Hispanic Devotional Piety: Tracing the Biblical Roots* (Maryknoll, NY: Orbis Books, 1991), esp., 32–33, 84–85.

[32] Romero, *Hispanic Devotional Piety,* 83.

theophanic manifestation of the divine presence. Doing theology sanjuanistamente enables us to interpret the bedroom *a lo divino*, and to see this place in the home as pregnant with possibilities for touching and savoring divine life.

Juan has been described as a mystic "whose psychological and religious make-up speak to traces of popular religion."[33] The popular imagination that reflected his Spanish Catholicism left an imprint on his ideas. As a Christian mystic, however, he rightly cautions against any form of idolatry, including idols connected with popular expressions of faith.[34] Any effort to understand his mysticism, his theology of God, and the way this theology taps into the experience of sexuality, must consider the incarnational nature of his spirituality and avoid turning any human experience into God. Returning the erotic to theology proceeds mindful of this premise. This effort affirms the integrity of human experiences yet ensures that human constructions never replace God. For this reason Juan's preferred speech of God is the poetic voice.

Mysticism and Poetry

Theology, as a number of theologians remind us, is not just related to content, but also to the forms of revelation.[35] In regard

---

[33] Federico Ruiz, *Místico y maestro, San Juan de la Cruz* (Madrid: Editorial de Espiritualidad, 1986), 79. Cited in Daniel de Pablo Maroto, "San Juan de la Cruz, Testigo de la Religiosidad Popular," *Salmanticensis* vol. 38, no.1 (1991): 65. Translation mine. For studies on sixteenth-century Spanish popular Catholicism, see Maroto, 73nn15, 16.

[34] See Maroto, "San Juan de la Cruz, Testigo de la Religiosidad Popular," 66; José Zurita Abril, "La religiosidad popular andaluza y San Juan de la Cruz," *Miriam* 43 (1991): 199–206.

[35] Theological aesthetics have been central to the development of Latin@ theology. Alejandro García-Rivera, *The Community of the Beautiful: A Theological Aesthetics* (Collegeville, MN: Liturgical Press, 1999); Roberto S. Goizueta, *Caminemos con Jesús: Toward a Hispanic/Latino*

to this argument Juan de la Cruz and Latinx theologians stand on common ground. What has been said with respect to Latinx theologians can equally be said with respect to Juan as a mystical theologian. His mind performs "in deep contact with myths, stories, traditions, and nature."[36] Juan argues, and any number of Latinx theologians might well agree, that poetry more than prose is a language better suited to express the ineffable mystery of God.

The theologian is not only an interpreter of faith experiences "but also its poet with unlimited possibilities for liberation and redemptive creativity."[37] As a poet, Juan captures in verse God's desire to liberate human persons from all unnecessary attachments that hold them back from participating in divine life. He uses the Spanish language to creatively unpack highly complex notions related to this process of purification and illumination that leads to knowing and uniting with God. Here, the ancient axiom, "*traduttore, traditore*" suggests why I have chosen to read Juan in Spanish, rather than in English translation. To avoid betraying his epistemological and theological ideas, doing theology sanjuanistamente means reading Juan in his native tongue. Without this reading, we simply miss out on some of the most important epistemological and theological insights that Juan's mystical theology has to offer.

The importance of the poetic word cannot be overemphasized. Although his commentaries provide doctrinal building blocks, Juan does not want them to limit interpretations of his poetry. In

---

Theology of Accompaniment (Maryknoll, NY: Orbis Books, 1995); Hans Urs von Balthasar, *The Glory of the Lord: A Theological Aesthetics*, vol. 1: *Seeing the Form*, trans. Erasmo Leiva-Merikakis, ed. John Riches (New York: T&T Clark, 1991).

[36] See Sixto J. García, "U.S. Hispanic and Mainstream Trinitarian Theologies," in *Frontiers of Hispanic Theology in the United States*, ed. Allan Figueroa Deck (Eugene, OR: Wipf and Stock, 2017 [originally published by Orbis Books,1992]), 93.

[37] García, "US Hispanic and Mainstream Trinitarian Theologies," 93.

this sense, his commentaries depend on his poems, but the poems do not depend on the commentaries.[38] Juan could not be clearer about the fact that his poems contain a surplus of meaning. And he invites us to consider other ways that the seductive power of divine love is at work in diverse men and women of faith:

> Since these songs were composed in love and in abundance of mystical understanding, *they are not intended to exhaust any understanding, nor is it my intention to do so.* My intention is only to shed some general light since your Reverence has so requested. I take this to be the better option since utterances of love are best left in their broadest sense so that one can benefit from them in accordance with the mode and capacity of their spirit rather than limiting them to one single meaning in a way that falls short of pleasing every palate. Thus, although some explanation is given to these stanzas, there is no need to bind ourselves to these understandings because mystical wisdom (which is given because of love and is the subject of these songs), need not be understood in any given way to effect love and affection in the soul, since it is in accordance with the mode of faith, that we love God without understanding him.[39]

Juan is not alone in opting for the poetic word and cautioning against the danger of theological discourse being abbreviated in ways that fail to include the faith experiences of particular persons and communities in relation to the life of God. Karl Rahner, one of the most influential trinitarian Catholic

---

[38] See Barnstone, *The Poetics of Ecstasy*, 174.

[39] CE, Prologo, 2. My emphasis added in italics. Juan wrote this commentary "Spiritual Canticle" upon the request of Madre Ana de Jesús, prioress of the Discalced Carmelite nuns of St. Joseph in Granada in 1584.

theologians of the twentieth century, also argued for the primordial function of the poetic word.[40] This mystic of everyday life, as he has been called, saw poetry as one step closer to expressing the mystery of God because of its open-ended nature.[41] Poetry, Rahner proposes, as opposed to doctrinal discourse, always contains a surplus of meaning. Poems invite us to ponder not only the ineffable mystery of God, but also the transcendental nature of human persons. Rational discourse, Rahner maintains, necessarily tends to abstraction, reification, limitation, and yes, as Juan would surely agree, even idolatry. The Spanish mystic and his German counterpart would probably concur that poetry, more than prose, draws us nearer to God and better safeguards the triune mystery. Rahner observes:

> And so it is true that the capacity and the practice of perceiving the poetic word is a presupposition to hearing the word of God. . . . The poetic word and the poetic ear are so much part of the human that if this essential power were really lost to the heart, man could no longer hear the word of God in the word of man. In its inmost essence, the poetic is a prerequisite for Christianity.[42]

Juan understood this essential function of poetry. His mystical theology presents the poetic word as the presupposition for hearing and succumbing to the seductive power of divine love. Doing theology sanjuanistamente summons us not to lose sight of this poetic word, and in the case of Juan's poems, be willing to sit

---

[40] See Robert Masson, "Rahner's Primordial Words and Bernstein's Metaphorical Leaps: The Affinity of Art with Religion and Theology," *Horizons* 33, no. 2 (Fall 2006): 276–297.

[41] See Egan, *Rahner, Mystic of Everyday Life*, 59.

[42] Karl Rahner, "Poetry and the Christian," in *Theological Investigations*, vol. 4, trans. Kevin Smyth (New York: Crossroad, 1982), 363.

and wrestle with them in efforts to unleash the human imagination and discover new theological interpretations.

Poetry remained for Juan his preferred means to express the mystery of God, and he wrote many other poems during and after this formative experience in his life, including "Living Flame of Love," which will be the main focus of this study. He hesitantly writes four commentaries that offer in prose great theological wisdom, but he cautions us to keep our imaginations wide open so the Spirit can bring about new interpretations in accordance with a plethora of human experiences and situations.

A Queer "y qué"

"The doctrine of the Trinity is ultimately a practical doctrine with radical consequences for Christian life."[43] Various contemporary theological voices reflect this premise in their efforts to relate divine and human life.[44] The same can be said of Latinx theological reflections on God, which highlight sociocultural and gender forms of oppression, practices that undermine human diversity and hybridity, and the experience of "community as the birthplace of the self."[45] In

---

[43] LaCugna, *God for Us*, 377.

[44] For instance, see Johnson, *She Who Is*; Phyllis Trible, *God and the Rhetoric of Sexuality* (Philadelphia: Fortress Press, 1978); M. Shawn Copeland, *Knowing Christ Crucified: The Witness of African American Religious Experience* (Maryknoll, NY: Orbis Books, 2018); James Cone, *The Cross and the Lynching Tree* (Maryknoll, NY: Orbis Books, 1970); Heup Young Kim, "The Tao in Confucianism and Taoism: The Trinity in East Asian Perspective," in *The Cambridge Companion to the Trinity* (Cambridge: Cambridge University Press, 2011), 293–308; Nancy L. Eiesland, *The Disabled God: Toward a Liberatory Theology of Disability* (Nashville, TN: Abingdon Press, 1994); Leonardo Boff, *Trinity and Society* (Maryknoll, NY: Orbis Books, 1988).

[45] See Miguel H. Díaz, "Life-Giving Migrations: Revisioning the Mystery of God through U.S. Hispanic Eyes," *Journal of Hispanic/Latino*

all of these explorations, we often find a focus on vanquished subjects and their experiences as *loci theologici* to encounter the triune life of God.[46] Often missing from these theological reflections is consideration of sexuality and the sexual subject.

Doing theology sanjuanistamente attends to this omission. Through his mystical poetry and prose Juan emerges as a welcome ally in efforts to denounce oppressive and idolatrous notions of God and to provide a more liberating and sexually informed theology of God.[47] The cornerstone of Juan's trinitarian theology is his theocentric orientation. This orientation relativizes and puts into human perspective all other human orientations, including sexual orienta-

---

Theology 11, no. 1 (2006): 20–40; idem, "A Trinitarian Approach to the Community-Building Process of Tradition: Oneness as Diversity in Christian Traditioning," in *Futuring Our Past: Explorations in the Theology of Tradition*, ed. Orlando O. Espín and Gary Macy (Maryknoll, NY: Orbis Books, 2006), 157–179; Alejandro García-Rivera, *The Community of the Beautiful* (Collegeville, MN: Liturgical Press, 1999); Gonzalez, *Created in God's Image*; Orlando O. Espín, "Trinitarian Monotheism and the Birth of Popular Catholicism," in *The Faith of the People*, 32–62; On the notion of "community as the birthplace of the self," see Goizueta, *Caminemos con Jesús*, 47–76.

[46] See Miguel H. Díaz, "On Loving Strangers: Encountering the Mystery of God in the Face of Migrants," in *Word & World* 29, no. 3 (2009): 234–242; Orlando O. Espín, "The God of the Vanquished: Foundations for a Latino Spirituality," in *The Faith of the People*, 11–31.

[47] For voices that have engaged Juan's thought from the perspective of Latin American liberation theology see, for instance, Segundo Galilea, *"San Juan de la Cruz y la espiritualidad liberadora," Medellín* 1 (1975): 216–222; idem, *El futuro de nuestro pasado. Ensayos sobre los místicos españoles desde America Latina* (New York: Northeast Catholic Pastoral Center for Hispanics, 1983); Michael Brundell, "The 'Liberation Theology' of John of the Cross," *Nubecula* 29 (1978): 41–44; Gustavo Gutiérrez, *"Juan de la Cruz desde America Latina," Selecciones de Teología* 32 (1993): 178–84; Guido Stinnesen, *"Saint Jean de la Croix: une mystique de liberation," Le Foi et le Temps* (1988): 571–584; Richard Hardy, "Liberation Theology and Saint John of the Cross: A Meeting," *Eglise e Théologie* 20 (1989): 259–282.

tions. Thus, Juan's spiritual and theological trinitarian insights have the power to dismantle gender- and sex-based oppressions. And when engaged in conversations with queer theologies, these insights further particularize the contribution his mystical theology makes to contents, contexts, and places from which God-talk arises.

Juan's mystical theology addresses these queer omissions with respect to an absence of sexuality that characterizes too many Catholic theologies, including Latinx theologies. Doing theology sanjuanistamente brings God out of theologically restrictive closets and enables our theologies of God to become more "catholic," particularly with respect to sexuality and marginalized queer sexual subjects. In 2003, James B. Nickoloff highlighted the queer omission in Latinx Catholic theologies. He cautioned: "It is queer that U.S. Latino/a theologians have not to date examined sexuality and sex with the same analytical rigor and commitment to justice which inform their theological appropriations of other dimensions of society, culture, and faith."[48] In 2007, Orlando O. Espín offered a similar observation:

> A number of Latina/o and black Catholic theologians have listed heterosexism and homophobia as evils symptomatic of wider and deeper social oppression. But most often, in our writings, these statements appear as part of longer lists of evil symptoms and not as the main focus of our papers, articles, or books. I am not disregarding or downplaying what has been written or said, but I don't think we can hold that a few phrases—no matter how accurate, passionate, and sincere—are sufficient. We have been mostly silent on the topic, at least within the world of the Catholic theological academy.[49]

---

[48] Nickoloff, "Sexuality: A Queer Omission," 50.
[49] Orlando O. Espín, *Grace and Humanness: Theological Reflections*

Engaging Juan's trinitarian theology and queering his theology breaks this silence. Walking in the footsteps of Juan, I take seriously the mystery of sexuality and, with him, see this mystery intrinsically oriented to God. Other theologians also share this view.[50] Reflecting en lo cotidiano, queer voices have underscored how "the everyday lives of people always provide us with a starting point for a process of doing a contextual theology without exclusions, in this case without the exclusion of sexuality struggling in the midst of misery."[51] In this way, writes Latin American theologian Marcella Althaus-Reid, queer theology confronts "the irruption of the sexual subject in history, in the same way that liberationists confronted the eruption of the Church of the poor or the 'underdogs of history.'"[52] In line with this irruption, queering Juan's mystical trini-

---

because of Culture (Maryknoll, NY: Orbis Books, 2007), 58. From the perspective of Latin American Liberation theology, see Claudio Carvalhaes, "Oppressed Bodies Don't Have Sex: The Blind Spots of Bodily and Sexual Discourses in the Construction of Subjectivity in Latin American Liberation Theology," in *Indecent Theologians: Marcella Althaus-Reid and The Next Generation of Post-Colonial Activism*, ed. Nicolas Panotto (Alameda, CA: Borderless Press, 2016), 157–158.

    [50] See, for instance, David H. Jensen, *God, Desire, and Sexuality* (Louisville, KY: Westminster John Knox Press, 2013); Linn Marie Tonstad, *God and Difference: The Trinity, Sexuality, and the Transformation of Finitude* (New York: Routledge, 2016); Rolf R. Nolasco Jr., *God's Beloved Queer: Identity, Spirituality and Practice* (Eugene, OR: Wipf & Stock, 2019); Gavin D'Costa, "Queer Trinity," in *Queer Theology: Rethinking the Western Body*, ed. Gerard Loughlin (Malden, MA: Blackwell, 2007), 269–280; Marcella Althaus-Reid, *The Queer God* (New York: Routledge Taylor & Francis Group, 2003); Stephen D. Moore, *God's Beauty Parlor and Other Queer Spaces in and around the Bible* (Stanford, CA: Stanford University Press, 2001); and Elaine Padilla, *Divine Enjoyment: A Theology of Passion and Exuberance* (New York: Fordham University Press, 2015).

    [51] Marcella Althaus-Reid, *Indecent Theology: Theological Perversions in Sex, Gender and Politics* (New York: Routledge, 2000), 4. See also Kelly, *Christian Mysticism's Queer Flame*.

    [52] Marcella Althaus-Reid, "On Queer Theory and Liberation

tarian theology repositions the Latinx option for culture to include the culture of the bedroom.[53]

Theology done latinamente, theology done sanjuanistamente, and theology done through queer eyes are all inherently practical. They engage lo cotidiano and seek to question norms and unmask idols that stand in the way of human participation in the life of God. Such theologizing prompts us to take seriously persons that have been marginalized from life-sustaining communal relationships, whether in their families, in their churches, or in public arenas. In turn, such questioning invites us to reconsider notions of the self in relationship to God and community. It reassesses issues of power, privilege, and human agency.[54] The words of Carmen Nanko-Fernández in reference to Latin@s theologians apply here as I re-think theology sanjuanistamente and queer this theology mindful of the marginalized and queer sexual subjects within our communities:

> Our past and contemporary experiences of marginaliza-
> tion have sensitized us to the dangers of privileging certain
> particularities and of inflating their significance with
> universal import. . . . Our contextual horizons charge us

Theology: The Irruption of the Sexual Subject in Theology," in *Homosexu-alities*, ed. Marcella Althaus-Reid, Regina Ammicht Quinn, Erik Borman, and Norbert Reck (London: SCM Press, 2008), 87.

[53] Orlando Espín and I first coined the phrase "the preferential option for culture" in *From the Heart of Our People*, 3. On the option for poor in Latin America see, Gustavo Gutíerrez, *A Theology of Liberation* (Maryknoll, NY: Orbis Books, 1971). On the option for the sexually marginalized poor, see Althaus-Reid, *Indecent Theology*. On the option for culture in Latinx theology, see first book of this Disruptive Cartographers series Miguel H. Díaz, ed., *The Word Became Culture* (Maryknoll, NY: Orbis Books, 2021), xv–xxix.

[54] Carmen Nanko-Fernández, *Theologizing en Espanglish: Context, Community, and Ministry* (Maryknoll, NY: Orbis Books, 2010), 19–20.

as theologians to question and critique current operative paradigms that fail to recognize diversity as constitutive of our human, national, and ecclesial conditions. Our contextual horizons invite us as theologians to pursue new directions for further explorations of diversity as these have ethical, practical, and pastoral implications.[55]

Retrieving and resourcing Latin@ theologies of God sanjuanistamente represent a new direction with ethical, practical, and pastoral implications, especially and preferentially with respect to queer Catholic persons.

As highlighted in this chapter, poetry is Juan's preferred language to speak "queerly" about God. It is a genre he uses to disrupt conventional understandings of God-talk, God's self-communication, and divine and human personhood. The next four chapters address these central themes common to trinitarian theology. Each of these chapters begins with a verse from his poem "Living Flame of Love."[56] I will use this poem and his prose commentary *Living Flame of Love* as springboards to explore his trinitarian theology. These writings open a window to see how Juan taps into the experience of human sexuality to convey God's seductive self-communication to human persons. Through Christ, our beloved spouse, and in the Holy Spirit, the living and divine flame of love, God makes room for us in the intimacy of the divine chambers.

---

[55] Nanko-Fernández, *Theologizing en Espanglish*, 20.

[56] In Spanish, the poem is titled "¡Llama de Amor Viva!" and the commentary, *Llama de Amor Viva*. For a bibliography on this poem and commentary, see "Llama de Amor Viva," in Manuel Diego Sánchez, *Bibliografía sistemática de San Juan de la Cruz* (Madrid: Editorial de Espiritualidad, 2000), 288–291, and for a bibliography of scholars that have studied the trinitarian nature of Juan's theology, see idem, "Doctrina trinitaria," 413–421.

2

DISRUPTING GOD-TALK

¡Oh llama de amor viva,
que tiernamente hieres
de mi alma en el más profundo centro!
Pues ya no eres esquiva,
Acaba ya, si quieres;
Rompe la tela de este dulce encuentro.[1]

Many contemporary Christian theologies disrupt traditional God-talk by tapping into diverse human experiences and embracing a wide range of methodological approaches.[2] They engage these experiences in critical conversations with the Bible, Christian traditions, and doctrines. These theologies retrieve, critique, and reconceive these sources in ways that liberate God-talk from the closet of limiting theological constructions. They offer possi-

---

[1] "O living flame of love, that tenderly wounds my soul in its deepest center, shy you are no more, do it now if you so will, break the veil of this sweet encounter." See the poem "Llama de Amor viva!" v. 1.

[2] See for instance, Elizabeth Johnson, *She Who Is: The Mystery of God in Feminist Theological Perspectives* (New York: Crossroad, 1992); Marcella Althaus-Reid, *The Queer God* (New York: Routledge, 2003); James Cone, *God of the Oppressed* (Maryknoll, NY: Orbis Books, 2003); Virgilio Elizondo, *Galilean Journey: The Mexican-American Promise* (Maryknoll, NY: Orbis Books, 2000); Leonardo Boff, *Trinity and Society* (Maryknoll, NY: Orbis Books, 1988).

bilities to think about God outside of the box: from new places, different persons, and diverse human experiences. Among other things, these theologies invite us to appreciate "the many colored veils through which divine mystery is mediated and by means of which we express relationship in return."[3]

Mystical experience is one of those veils through which divine mystery is mediated. Karl Rahner proposed that to be human is to be mystical. He once commented that the Christian of the future will be a mystic or would cease being a Christian at all.[4] As Rahner used the term, mysticism refers to the fact that "all personal experiences contain at least an implicit, yet primordial, experience of God."[5] Human persons are, at their core, religious and graced creatures who are constantly "on the lookout for a human word in which God's word can be revealed."[6]

The words that our restless hearts seek in order to name our encounters with God are necessarily shaped by human contexts and experiences, yet no human word should ever be turned into an idol.[7] At the same time, human language should not be dismissed as a mediator of the human encounter with God. The mystical theology

---

[3] Johnson, *She Who Is*, 46. See also Elizabeth A. Johnson, *Quest for the Living God: Mapping Frontiers in the Theology of God* (New York: Continuum, 2007); Miguel H. Díaz, "The Word That Crosses: Life-Giving Encounters with the Markan Jesus and Guadalupe," in *The Word Became Culture*, ed. Miguel H. Díaz (Maryknoll, NY: Orbis Books, 2021), 1–24.

[4] See Karl Rahner, "Christian Living Formerly and Today," in *Theological Investigations VII*, trans. David Bourke (New York: Herder and Herder, 1971), 15. See also Harvey D. Egan, *Karl Rahner, Mystic of Everyday Life* (New York: Crossroad, 1998), 57.

[5] Egan, *Karl Rahner, Mystic of Everyday Life*, 57.

[6] Stephen J. Duffy, *The Dynamics of Grace: Perspectives in Theological Anthropology* (Collegeville, MN: Liturgical Press, 1993), 269.

[7] See Miguel H. Díaz, *On Being Human: U.S. Hispanic and Rahnerian Perspectives* (Maryknoll, NY: Orbis Books, 2001), esp. 94–96, 117–128.

of Juan de la Cruz opens a theological horizon to understand not only mystical experience itself but also the potential of human sexuality to offer insight into the triune mystery of divine love.[8]

Framing God-talk according to the language of human sexuality affirms the omnipresence of God in human experience. A turn to mystical union, and the way Juan taps into the analogue of human sexuality, helps us rethink God-talk. Juan's mystical theology invites us to consider how in Christ we come to know God intimately as our spouse, similar to how spouses come "to know" one another in love. Love, or to be more precise, the love of the Spirit, makes knowing of divine and human persons possible. The Spirit, as God's living flame, not only unites us to God, but the Spirit also unites us to one another, enabling us to know God and one another in love.[9]

Turning to the bedroom shifts our focus to a space that Juan crafts metaphorically to situate the loving relationship that takes place between divine and human persons in mystical union. Using a metaphor that evokes an embodied way of knowing challenges typical ways of understanding mystical union.

Option for the Bedroom and Human Sexuality

Using vivid images, including the bedroom, that evoke courtship and the intimacy of sexual union, Juan often portrays God as a Lover who pursues the beloved for the sake of union.[10] This

---

[8] See Willis Barnstone, "Mystico-Erotic Love 'O Living Flame of Love,'" *Revista Hispánica Moderna* 37, no. 4 (1972–73): 253–261.

[9] "*Sintomáticamente, 'llama' es tanto el Espíritu Santo como el amor del hombre . . . La imagen de la 'llama', que es aire (humano) y fuego (divino), le parece al poeta excelente portadora de esta intuición simbólica de la compenetración entre la actividad humana y divina.*" See Gabriel Castro, "Llama de Amor Viva," *Introducción a la lectura de San Juan de la Cruz*, ed. Agustín García Simón (Salamanca, ES: Junta de Castilla y León, 1991): 518.

[10] A word about the use of the term "beloved" in this chapter. When capitalized (Beloved), it will refer to Christ, when it appears in lowercase it

Lover-God who unites with humanity in Jesus Christ, wills for
the Spirit (whom Juan identifies as God's living flame of Love) to
"break the veil" ("*rompe la tela de este dulce encuentro*") that separates divine and human life so that human persons may enter the
divine chamber and partake of its benefits.[11] In many ways, this
sixteenth-century mystic is ahead of his times, anticipating the
suggestion by Marcella Althaus-Reid that the bedroom is an appropriate vantage point from which to rethink God-talk.[12]

In 1983, Willis Barnstone noted that "all commentary within
the Spanish world has denied the immediate level of the love
experience in Saint John's love poetry."[13] While I am not certain
about "all," this observation underscores a curious omission given
the historical literary and religious heritage of Muslim Spain
that had influenced even the contexts that shaped Juan's identity
as a Spanish mystic long after the Convivencia. The argument
that Juan's poetry derives from Italian, Spanish, Portuguese, and

---

refers to human persons as Christ's beloved. As verse 5 of the poem "Noche
Oscura" exemplifies, both uses are common to Juan: "*amado*" (Christ, the
Beloved) con "*amada*" (beloved, the personified soul)—"*amada con el
amado transformada.*" At times Juan uses the term "beloved" to mean "my
darling." See chapter 8 of George H. Tavard, *Poetry and Contemplation in
St. John of the Cross* (Athens: Ohio University, 1988), 137–157.

   [11] On the theological and sexual connotations of this expression, see
Barnstone, "Mystico-Erotic Love," 253–261; Ian Macpherson, "Rompe
la tela de este dulce encuentro: San Juan's 'Llama de amor viva' and the
Courtly Context," in *Studies in Honor of Bruce W. Wardropper*, ed. Dian
Fox, Harry Sieber, and Robert TerHorst (Newark, DE: Juan de la Cuesta,
1989),193–203.

   [12] See Marcella Althaus-Reid, "On Queer Theory and Liberation
Theology: The Irruption of the Sexual Subject in Theology," in *Homosexu-
alities*, ed. Marcella Althaus-Reid, Regina Ammicht Quinn, Erik Borgman,
and Norbert Reck (London: SCM Press, 2008), 87.

   [13] Willis Barnstone, *The Poetics of Ecstasy: Varieties of Ekstasis from
Sappho to Borges* (New York: Holmes & Meier, 1983), 182.

Hebrew sources, while accurate, is not sufficient.[14] Juan is heir
to a long and well-established literary tradition of love poems in
Al-Andalus, as Muslim Iberia was known for centuries. In this
tradition, explicitly religious literature, and other forms of literature, especially dealing with the subject of love, interacted, and
affected one another. For instance, a number of Iberian poets from
this period were also religious scholars who presented "readers with
a subversive yet sublime message about the nature and power of
romantic human love."[15] We should not be surprised then to see
Juan reflecting this rich tradition from Al-Andalus in his presentation of erotic love *a lo divino*.

Juan's poems depict a loving tenderness between God and
human persons, in ways that bind their hearts and unite them as one.

> *O guiding night! O night more beautiful than the dawn,*
> *O night that joined together*
> *Lover and beloved joined as one.*
> *Transforming each of them into the other.*
>
> *Upon my flowering chest which I kept for him alone*
> *There he fell asleep,*
> *And I caressing him . . .*
>
> *I parted his hair,*
> *And with his gentle hand, he wounded my neck*
> *Suspending all my senses . . .*[16]

---

[14] On the sourcing of Juan's poems, see Barnstone, *The Poetics of Ecstasy*, 163–167.

[15] Shari L. Lowin, *Arabic and Hebrew Love Poems in Al-Andalus* (New York: Routledge Taylor & Francis Group, 2014), 102.

[16] "Noche Oscura," vv. 5–7. See also N, 1.1–5.

There is no denying the sensuality evident in these verses from "The Dark Night." Barnstone observes, and I concur, that "there is no need to deprive the lovers in his poems of their bodies, of their embraces, their sexuality, their physical ecstasy, in order to read the poems as mystical tracts." Barnstone insists that "San Juan is not shy, coy, or elusive" in his descriptions of love.[17] Rather he is "direct, devoid of shame, buoyantly intense in describing the sexual act."[18] Juan's turn to experiences of human sexuality to frame mystical union with Christ is not simply a literary ploy. His mystical theology is deeply incarnational. This language of love conveys a spiritual union that vividly reflects the type of intimacy found in the arms of lovers.

Read from the perspective of the Catholic analogical imagination, these metaphors suggest that human sexuality can help us appreciate trinitarian divine interpersonal relationships.[19] Juan invites us to consider, consistent with a sixteenth-century Iberian worldview, the profound religious nature of human sexuality. Affirming a relationship of similarity-in-difference between mystical and sexual union, makes explicit the bedroom and human sexuality as *loci theologici*.

At the core of Juan's theology of God is the praxis of intimate and interpersonal love defined by actions, reactions, and mutual self-giving between divine and human persons.[20] This divine praxis, however, is one that mirrors human love actions and reactions, and mutual acts of self-giving that are in themselves deeply religious experiences. Here, the following observations regarding the cultural and religious influences of medieval Spain are worth noting, especially given the *converso* background of this Iberian mystic's family:

---

[17] Barnstone, *The Poetics of Ecstasy*, 182.

[18] Barnstone, *The Poetics of Ecstasy*, 182.

[19] See David Tracy, *The Analogical Imagination: Christian Theology and the Culture of Pluralism* (New York: Crossroad, 1998).

[20] See Castro, "Llama de Amor Viva," 518.

It has become almost axiomatic to note that many religious traditions teach that to be closer to God, one must distance oneself from the pull of the sensual world. It is thus puzzling to the modern mind to find Muslim and Jewish scholars of religion, authority figures in their faiths, standing proudly among the greatest composers of erotic secular love poetry in Muslim Spain of the tenth to thirteenth century. After all, we do not generally find imams or rabbis among the prime proponents of indulgence in physical pleasures. Yet, in Muslim Spain, rather than separating the spiritual world from the physical world, distinguishing between what the modern world deems the secular and the religious realms, these Muslim and Jewish religious authority figures fused the two.[21]

Juan did not write his poems and commentaries only for celibate and chaste religious men and women. He also wrote for lay persons, perhaps more likely to connect and draw deep spiritual insights from their particular and lived sexual experiences. Consider that it was a widowed woman who asked Juan to write the commentary on his poem "Living Flame of Love."[22] His decision to accept this commission demonstrates that Juan envisioned a more inclusive audience for his mystical theology beyond his vowed religious community.[23]

---

[21] Lowin, *Arabic and Hebrew Love Poems in Al-Andalus*, 1.

[22] Llama, Prologo, 1n1, in *Obra completa,* vol. 2, 245n2. See also Castro, "Llama de Amor Viva," 494–495.

[23] "The fact that John wrote this work for a laywoman, his friend and penitent Doña Ana de Peñalosa, shows that he did not think that the heights of mystical union were restricted to cloistered men and women." See Bernard McGinn, *Mysticism in the Golden Age of Spain (1500–1650)*, vol. 6, part 2, of *The Presence of God: A History of Western Christian Mysticism* (New York: Crossroad, 2017), 302.

In his poetry, Juan appeals to the night, to human desire, to pain and pleasure. He uses flames to express love and to convey divine touch. He is not alone because other poets, mystics, and religious writers in Spain had drawn on similar images and themes to relate human and divine life.[24] To ignore the sensuality of phrases like "*rompe la tela de este dulce encuentro*" is to strip them of their profoundly spiritual meaning. In this case, the phrase connotes both the desire of human lovers to eliminate whatever keeps them from consummating their human love, as well as the desire to eliminate whatever keeps us from the consuming and consummating union with God.[25]

Juan describes the place of encounter with God both as his flowering chest, "*en mi pecho florido,*"[26] and as the bed he shares with Christ, "*nuestro lecho florido.*"[27] In his commentary on "The Spiritual Canticle," Juan tells us that this bed is none other than Christ, his spouse, "*Porque el lecho no es otra cosa que su mismo Esposo el verbo Hijo de Dios . . . en el cual ella por medio de la dicha union de Amor se recuesta.*"[28] In effect the soul does not only lie down on the flowery bed but on the flower itself which is the Son of God.[29] In Juan's writings, as in those of other Christian mystics, the bed is a symbol of love, the place of the nuptial union between Christ and the soul.[30]

We should not dismiss the sensuality of this metaphor or the spiritual significance of sexual union associated with this place of human intimacy. As Gerard Loughlin notes, employing marriage

---

[24] See Lowin, *Arabic and Hebrew Love Poems in Al-Andalus,* esp. 88–90, 153–154, 167; 257–273.

[25] Llama, 1.29–36.

[26] "Noche Oscura," v. 6.

[27] "Cántico Espiritual," v. 15.

[28] CE, 24.1.

[29] CE, 24.1.

[30] Tavard, *Poetry and Contemplation in St. John of the Cross,* 45.

as a metaphor for the spiritual relationship between Christ and the soul does not lessen its sexual connection: "The marital relationship is no less sexual for being spiritualized."[31]

Appreciating the metaphor of the bedroom calls for recognizing the distinction between the mystical and the sexual. Conflating the two runs the risk of idolizing the human experience of sexuality and of erasing legitimate differences between the two realms. Failure to distinguish between the relationship of divine and human persons in mystical union, on the one hand, and the relationship between human persons in sexual union, on the other, would run counter to the theocentric vision of Juan's mystical theology. At the same time, Juan's trinitarian theology calls for integration rather than separation of the mystical and the sexual.

Christopher Hinkle proposes that "erotic desire (and practice) can and should serve God, but this requires significant internal renovation, a stripping away perhaps even of those elements which at first seemed conducive to relationship with the transcendent."[32] Still, as he underscores, "The goal of disciplining sensual desire and distinguishing it is eventually to bring it more fully into alignment with desire for God such that we, upon 'feeling the delight of certain tastes and delicate touches, immediately at the first movement direct [our] thought and the affection of [our] will to God . . . *that he be more known and loved through them*.'"[33]

The imagery of the bedroom is entirely appropriate to express God's triune life. Juan's option for the bedroom anticipates some contemporary theologians who have given significant attention to the bedroom as a place of human encounter with God. Marcella

---

[31] Gerard Loughlin, introduction to *Queer Theology: Rethinking the Western Body*, ed. Gerard Loughlin (Malden, MA: Blackwell, 2007), 6. Emphasis in original.

[32] Christopher Hinkle, "Love's Urgent Longings," in *Queer Theology*, 195.

[33] Hinkle, "Love's Urgent Longings," 195. Emphasis added.

Althaus-Reid contends that because of the irruption of the sexual subject into history, "Suddenly theology does not take place in the university or seminary but in the bedroom."[34] Relocating the place for theological reflection to the bedroom and turning to the experience of sexuality to inform theologizing on the triune God carry epistemological implications. The parallel between knowing God in a sensual sense of the term and the sexual "knowing" that occurs with lovers is one that now leads us to explore Juan's embodied epistemology.

On Knowing God

In part 1 of the *Summa theologiae* (*Prima Pars*), Thomas Aquinas reflects on the nature of God, the knowledge of God, and the way human persons can name the reality of God. Particularly relevant to our exploration of Juan's trinitarian musings are questions 12–13 on knowing and naming God in the section *De Deo Uno*, and questions 29–32 on naming and knowing the divine persons in *De Deo Trino*. In questions 12–13, Thomas draws from his central teaching on the analogy of being to argue that we know God from God's creation, that is, from God's "effects." Catherine LaCugna posits that for Thomas, "Naming God must conform to the way we know God; we know God on the basis of creatures since we are unable to know God's essence directly."[35] In other words, we cannot know *what* God is, only *that* God is.

Whereas questions 12–13 of the *Summa* focus on rationally knowing and naming the one God through God's effects (creaturely mediation), questions 29–32 reverse the order of knowledge and focus on the revelation of the triune God. The reason for this

---

[34] Althaus-Reid, *The Queer God*, 29.

[35] Catherine M. LaCugna, *God for Us: The Trinity & Christian Life* (New York: HarperCollins, 1991), 151.

reversal is that for Thomas, humans have no way to know that God is *triune* outside of revelation. In these questions, Thomas invites us to consider how revelation tells us something about God's triune life itself, rather than knowing by way of reason the one God from God's effects on creation. Thus, that God exists and is one can be reasonably ascertained from the effects of God's actions upon creation (qq. 2–26). This premise gets played out in Thomas's five proofs related to God's existence. That God is triune, however, we can know only from revelation. Thus questions 29–32 present an epistemology that proceeds from naming the triune God revealed in Scripture to knowing this triune mystery. LaCugna succinctly summarizes this epistemology in the following way:

> Question 32 establishes the basis for knowledge of the divine persons. Reason alone could not lead to knowledge that God is a Trinity of persons. This may appear to conflict with the principle established in question 12 that we know God on the basis of the created world. We know *the one* God on the basis of creation but *we do not know the Trinity* on this basis. On the basis of reason we know that the one God is the source of beings. And, since God's causality toward creation as Creator is exercised in common by all three persons (Thomas is following Augustine's principle, *opera trinitatis ad extra indivisa sunt*), there is no rational basis for differentiating persons within God. Revelation alone gives this knowledge.[36]

In his mystical theology, Juan integrates this way of knowing the one God through reason with knowing the triune God through revelation. It is the triune God who intimately communicates with and desires to unite with human persons. While Juan does

---

[36] LaCugna, *God for Us,* 152.

not contradict Thomas, his mysticism offers a more intimate and personal way of knowing God, an epistemology that proceeds by way of love.[37]

In mystical experience human persons enter into a relationship with the triune God to engage the deepest part of their embodied selves and produce a knowing that arises from within the very life of God.[38] Such intimacy with God allows people to know God not as an object in the world of experience but in a personal way. According to Howells,

> John uses the word "object" here of God in relation to the spiritual faculties, in spite of the possible confusion with the objects of the senses. He says that the spiritual faculties are perfected in regard to their spiritual objects (*objetos*), which are the persons of the Trinity: the will in regard to the Holy Spirit, the intellect to the Son, and the memory to the Father. By no means does he wish to suggest that God becomes known in the manner of ordinary objects

---

[37] Juan writes: "*Y así espero que, aunque se escriban aquí algunos puntos de teología escolástica acerca del trato interior del alma con su Dios, no será en vano haber hablado algo a lo puro del espíritu en tal manera; pues, aunque a Vuestra Reverencia le falte el ejercicio de teología escolástica, con que se entienden las verdades divinas, no le falta el de la mística, que se sabe por amor, en lo que no solamente se saben, mas justamente se gustan.* [And I hope that although I will write about some scholastic theological principles concerning the subject of the soul's intimacy with God, it will not be in vain to speak of the spirit in such a lofty manner, even though your Reverence lacks training in scholastic theology through which one understands divine truth, you do not lack mystical understanding through which one knows by the way of love, in which one not only knows but also savors.]" In Prologue, CE, 3.

[38] See Edward Howells, *John of the Cross and Teresa of Avila: Mystical Knowing and Selfhood* (New York: Crossroad, 2002), 51. See also Ruth Burrows, *Ascent to Love: The Spiritual Teaching of St. John of the Cross* (Denville, NJ: Dimensions, 1987), 91–113.

of the senses; rather, he uses the word "object" in the sense of the *relationship* between these faculties and the Trinity which is now becoming explicit. The soul is beginning to recognize the persons of the Trinity as its partners in this relationship rather than as objects in the normal sense. Nevertheless, they are objects in that they are *other* than the soul and are now recognized in their essence for the first time: not just as the depth of the soul but as a *relationship* with God at this deep level which the soul is becoming able to differentiate more and more clearly.[39]

With respect to mystical knowledge, Juan stresses human transformation as the possibility for radical mutuality, commensurability, and equality between divine and human persons. "The soul in order to know something, must become like the object of its knowledge."[40] Mystical experience, and in particular mystical union, precipitates the condition that allows human persons to participate in this kind of knowing. Juan offers a different kind of knowing God, a kind of knowing beyond the one most of us normally associate with rational knowledge or with revelation.

Juan does not deny the Catholic understanding that knowledge of God comes from the senses.[41] Still, Juan cautions us against knowing that relies on our unpurified senses (bodily and spiritual). Juan maintains that in our "natural" state we stand disoriented and attached to worldly realities, rather than oriented and attached to God. This is why in this natural state, we lack the kind of knowing that is commensurate with knowing the divine persons. The mystical journey sets into motion the conditions of the possibility of knowing God. It establishes the condition that makes not only

---

[39] Howells, *John of the Cross and Teresa of Avila*, 51–52.
[40] Howells, *John of the Cross and Teresa of Avila*, 18.
[41] Howells, *John of the Cross and Teresa of Avila*, 18–19.

knowing possible but, more important, makes union with God possible. Mystical union creates a "union of likeness," "*unión de semejanza.*" Here Juan follows the scholastic principle that states, "Whatever is received can only be received in accordance with the mode of the receiver."[42]

Juan's epistemology resonates with sexual ways of knowing. His mystical theology presents us with an embodied way of knowing God oftentimes missing from contemporary discourse on God with the notable exception of Latinx theologies. To know Christ is to know God, and Latinx theologians have emphasized that to know Christ involves personal and communal accompaniment; however, the sexual dimension remains a lacuna.[43] Like mystical knowledge, the knowing that takes place between lovers is not achieved through the exercise of disembodied reason. It is instead savored in and through their love.[44] Knowing is relational and embodied. Juan invites us to consider how knowledge of God through mystical union, in both its apophatic and cataphatic dimensions, can be described in the language of sexual union.

The Apophatic Way: On the Dark Night of Knowing

Knowing God calls for detachment. For Juan, knowing calls for the darkening of our spiritual and bodily senses through what he describes as active and passive nights.[45] This means detaching not

---

[42] "*Quidquid accipitur, accipitur secundum modum accipientis.*" See Llama, 2, 34. See Howells's discussion of this principle in *John of the Cross and Teresa of Avila*, 18–19.

[43] See Roberto S. Goizueta, *Caminemos con Jesús: Toward a Hispanic/Latino Theology of Accompaniment* (Maryknoll, NY: Orbis Books, 1995), 140–162.

[44] CE, Prologo, 3.

[45] See Burrows, *Ascent to Love*, 49–57, 69–78, 106–117.

only our minds but also our will from all that is not God. Since Juan holds that union and knowledge of God lie beyond our natural capacity, God must reorder our natural selves to establish commensurability between divine and human life. Detachment is essential to achieve this commensurability. It is not our human effort alone to achieve, but a graced human praxis that can require us to act in ways that may be contrary to what is natural, constructed, and accepted as normal. According to Juan, failing to undertake this disruptive and purgative journey is what keeps us from climbing the mountain of love on the way to union and knowledge of God.[46]

Juan speaks in paradoxes, but we must be careful not to misinterpret his tendency to utilize dichotomies, that is, what Burrows calls his "lack of shading."[47] We must detach from worldly realities to become attached to God. We must strip ourselves of human constructs in order to truly know God.[48] We must enter into the dark night to experience and know God. Darkness, Juan tells us, paradoxically translates into enlightenment. Enlightenment in divine love, in turn, leads to knowing God and one another. The blinding splendor of divine love must darken our spiritual and bodily senses if we desire to see as God sees the world. This paradoxical God-talk bears enormous relevance. Without this way of negation, we are seduced by false loves and prone to live in ignorance. Religiously constructed misunderstandings of God can often be harmful and can get in the way of knowledge of and union with God. According to Juan, the highest degree of knowledge is attained when we let go of all that is not God and allow God to secretly teach us in the perfection of love. He writes:

---

[46] See Burrows, *Ascent to Love*, 72–73.

[47] See Burrows, *Ascent to Love*, 93.

[48] See McGinn, *Mysticism in the Golden Age of Spain*, 268.

The dark night is God acting on the soul, purifying the soul of all ignorance and habitual imperfections, whether they be natural or spiritual. This, contemplatives call infused contemplation or mystical theology through which God secretly teaches souls and instructs them in the perfection of love, without their assistance or understanding.[49]

The night is experienced as a dimming of our intellectual vision, a cleansing of our memories, and a reordering of our will to desire nothing less than God. Juan affirms:

Since these natural faculties lack purity, strength, and the capacity to be able to receive and taste the supernatural things according to their condition, which is divine, but can only receive according to their human and lowly condition, it's best that they be darkened. . . . Thus once these faculties and appetites of the soul have been tempered, they can receive, feel, and taste, what is divine and supernatural, which is inconceivable until the old man dies.[50]

The issue for Juan is not the body, its spiritual and its bodily senses per se. It is the personal and social disorientation through the senses that can keep us from knowing God.

The dark night clears human vision to know as God knows. Juan writes, "The intellect, which before union with God understood naturally with the force and energy of its natural light through sensorial corporal means, moved and showered by the higher principle of God's supernatural light, becomes one with God and thereby participates in divine knowing."[51] Juan maintains

---

[49] N, 2, 5.1.
[50] N, 2, 16.4.
[51] Llama, 2.34.

that whereas in its natural and sensorial state, knowledge precedes love; in its spiritual state, love precedes knowledge. The soul infused by the presence and love of God becomes oriented to God, participates in God, and therefore, knows God in love.[52]

Once again, we can trace a link between Juan's theocentric epistemology and human sexuality. In human intimacy, detachment and self-surrender are ways to unite and know another. Juan puts an emphasis on darkening our senses, letting go, and surrendering to divine love as a way to know God. In this way the mystic's knowledge of God does not lead to possession but rather to recognition of the mystery of God. Similarly, the knowledge gained through non-exploitative sexual love culminates with the affirmation that one's beloved is not a possession for material consumption. As Mark Jordan argues, "The highest moment of mystical union is a *nocturnal encounter* with the beloved who in that moment eludes our expectation."[53] This is also the case with erotic union, "As soon as the lover is claimed as fully known, we have lost the lover and the lover's gift of pleasure."[54]

Juan's apophatic approach calls for radical detachment from all worldly experiences that keep us from uniting and knowing God. This includes letting go of unhealthy distractions connected to money, power, and privilege. In this sense, Juan's spirituality implies that we consider and reject not only personal but also social obstacles that stand in the way of God.[55] Although it is true that Juan's mysticism does not explicitly address political and economic obstacles that distort human encounters with God, this does not mean that his mystical theology is irrelevant on these

---

[52] CE, 26.8–10.

[53] Mark Jordan, *The Ethics of Love* (Malden, MA: Blackwell, 2002), 166. Emphasis added.

[54] Jordan, *The Ethics of Love*, 166.

[55] Gustavo Gutiérrez, *A Theology of Liberation* (Maryknoll, NY: Orbis Books, 1988), 165–173.

issues. In the words of Gustavo Gutiérrez, "The night of the senses and the spiritual night ought to strip us, and finally liberate us, from idolatries."[56] Money, privilege, and power, which shape our personal and social constructions of God, can all too easily lead us to succumb to idolatry. The ascent to love that Juan's mysticism demands does not represent an escape from the world or a leap "beyond ethical-political" responsibility, but instead represents "a leap into ethical political action," especially on behalf of the marginalized and the poor.[57]

The Cataphatic Way of Knowing God

Juan is not just a theologian who negates, but he is a theologian who affirms. This is especially the case in his poem and commentary on the "Living Flame of Love." A close look at Juan's writings shows how his use of Spanish indicates that mystical knowing is not a mere exercise of the mind, but an embodied and relational experience. Knowing God and knowing persons entails interpersonal accompaniment. Juan invites us to understand accompaniment with images that are associated with the intimacy of human sexuality. The kind of knowing that takes place in sexual activity is described well in Goizueta's discussion of aesthetic praxis rooted in empathic love.

> To relate to another as a person, I must "fuse" with him or her, that is we must enter into each other not only as physical bodies—though, as we will see, this will also be

---

[56] Daniel G. Groody, *Gustavo Gutiérrez: Spiritual Writings* (Maryknoll, NY: Orbis Books, 2011), 223–224.

[57] Here, I am indebted to Goizueta who makes this observation in terms of love and the sociopolitical factors that mediate love and relationship with others. See Roberto S. Goizueta, "*La raza cósmica?* The Vision of Vasconcelos," *Journal of Hispanic/Latino Theology* 1, no. 2 (1994): 24. See also idem, *Caminemos con Jesús*, 101–131.

essential—but as whole human beings. Thus, the only way we can "fuse" with each other is affectively, through empathy—in the same way as we "fuse" with a beautiful sunrise, or a beautiful piece of music. We can know objects through observation and logical analysis, but we can only know human persons through empathic love.[58]

To illustrate this understanding of knowing in Juan's writings, let us consider the significance of some Spanish verbs used in his poems to describe divine and human actions.[59] These verbs provide evidence that Juan's emphasis on knowing through negation does not represent a denial of the senses and the body but an invitation to reorient and expand our senses to truly enjoy God and God's creation.[60] For instance, consider how verbs like *saber* ("to know, to taste"), *gustar* ("to delight"), and *tocar* ("to touch") convey a deeply embodied epistemology.

In the poem "Living Flame of Love," Juan speaks of God's delicate touch and the human ability to taste eternity through this touch (*"que a vida eterna sabe"*).[61] As a Christian mystic, Juan uses this language to evoke an incarnational experience of God. Juan suggests an embodied sense of knowing God through his use of the Spanish verb *"saber,"* because *saber* can be rendered in English both as "to know" and "to taste." The God Christianity proclaims

---

[58] Goizueta, *Caminemos con Jesús*, 92.

[59] See the classic study by Dámaso Alonso, *La poesía de San Juan de la Cruz* (Madrid: Aguilar, 1966).

[60] Denys Turner argues that it is reasonable to qualify the apophatic statements that Juan makes, like the claim that the soul's mere love of something prevents it from union and transformation in God (S 1, 4, 3) as the equivalent of a literary (and I would add, theological) ellipsis, and as one would do in Eckhart, read Juan's notion of desire and appetite as referring to "possessive appetites." *The Darkness of God: Negativity in Christian Mysticism* (Cambridge: Cambridge University Press, 1995), 233.

[61] "Llama," v. 2.

is a God who becomes flesh and is known in the flesh. Juan insists that knowledge of eternal truths is embodied and not some kind of mere rational exercise. By using *saber*, Juan affirms that knowledge of God delights our senses. Spirituality does not sever the mind from the body or knowledge of God from the senses.

To taste, to touch, to delight—these verbs convey multisensory engagement and intimacy.[62] The very process of sensorial purification, which strips us from all that is not God, does not result in an escape from the body but rather a deeper integration of our spiritual and bodily reality. This is why Juan's pervasive apophatic arguments cannot be used as basis for claiming a purely spiritual and disembodied theological anthropology or way of knowing divine and human realities. Juan's epistemology is not anti-body even if he never ceases to remind us of the imperative to darken our senses and turn away from the seductions of the material world. His concern is with avoiding false attachments and emphasizing instead our capacity to grow in divine love.

Juan sketches two ways of knowing, the first of which is more evident at the beginning of our ascent to divine love, and the second associated with the more advanced stages of this spiritual journey. At the summit of love, in mystical union the sensory and spiritual ways of knowing are fully integrated. In mystical union, we witness the "trinitarian dynamism that draws the soul forward in mystical transformation, instilling the structure of the Trinity without removing, but rather purging and perfecting, its natural cognitive structure."[63]

---

[62] See Mary Paul Cutri, O.C.D, "The Touch of God: Human/Divine Intimacy," *Spiritual Life* 30 (1984): 157–162. Juan uses the metaphor of "touch" in the singular and plural. When used in the singular, it tends to carry a Christological connection; in the plural it carries a pneumatological connection. In all cases, it depicts God's intimate relationship with human persons. See Llama, 2.16–20, 1.35.

[63] Howells, *John of the Cross and Teresa of Avila*, 39.

At these advanced spiritual states, God's light outshines all other ways of knowing so that we might know as God knows. In this respect we can speak of a knowledge of God that is not primarily dependent on our senses (*sine media creatura*).[64] As he writes of this advanced spiritual stage, Juan continues to turn to language that conveys a profound embodied and sensual experience of God. The phrase "tasting eternity" is found in Juan's poem "Living Flame of Love." This poem primarily addresses this final stage of union. Juan chooses this phrase to capture this climactic moment of mystical union. "*Rompe la tela de este dulce encuentro*," he tells us, that is, let God's living flame of love break open the veil that keeps divine and human persons from fusing and uniting with one another. God's living flame of love consumes and consummates a spiritual-bodily communion. Thus through mystical experience we are led to savor the eternal God, "*que a vida eterna sabe*."[65]

Juan's poetic playfulness disrupts our sanitized Christian epistemologies that are too often afraid to pay attention to the ways that sexual relationships can inform our understanding of the mystery of God. Barnstone picks up on the *synesthetic* significance conveyed by *saber* in the phrase, "*que a vida eterna sabe*" ("tasting of eternal life"). He proposes that the use of *saber* creates a synesthetic ambiguity[66] that "revives the ancient lexical complexity of the Latin verb *sapere,* meaning 'to know,' 'to have wisdom,'" adding "a cognitive undertone to a sensorial verb, effectively conveying both the physical and intellectual experience."[67]

Still, more precision can be added with respect to the cognitive undertones of *saber.* "Living Flame of Love" is about sexual love, and there is no way to get around it. It is a love poem that

---

[64] On the role of the corporeal senses in knowing spiritual realities, see Howells, *John of the Cross and Teresa of Avila*, 34–39, 55–59.

[65] "Llama," v. 1.

[66] Barnstone, *The Poetics of Ecstasy,* 186.

[67] Barnstone, *The Poetics of Ecstasy,* 186.

uses courtship and erotic language to express communion between
divine and human persons.[68] That *saber* contains an erotic undertone can be further demonstrated when we consider other places
where Juan uses this verb. For instance, in his poem "The Dark
Night" Juan speaks of the fire of love caused by his pulsating heart
that guides him to meet his lover, a lover he tells us that he knew so
well, "*a quien yo bien me sabia.*"[69] It is hard to imagine that Juan was
not aware of the sexual content of his writings. Speaking of "Living
Flame of Love," Barnstone writes,

> In San Juan's poem, we are dealing not only with the logic
> of a consistent symbolism but with a specific description
> of the act of love. The author means and is aware of what
> he is saying. It is inconceivable that he could have written
> so beautifully and explicitly about tender and ecstatic
> physical love without understanding his own words. If he
> did so, then we are dealing with miracles and madness. Yet,
> in the end, even Juan's awareness is irrelevant. For we, as
> readers, have the text before us and that is sufficient. The
> use of any external apparatus to blind us from the literal
> text is an error.[70]

That Juan was aware of the sexual content of his writings would
be among the reasonable explanations given his familiarity with
the biblical tradition in which knowing can refer to intimacy and
sexual union (Genesis 4:17: Cain "knew" his wife).[71] In turning

---

[68] "*¡O cauterio suave! ¡Oh mano blanda! ¡O toque delicado, que a vida
eterna sabe, y toda deuda paga!* [O gentle cautery! O soft hand! O delicate
touch, that tastes of eternity and pays all debt]". "Llama," v. 2.

[69] "Noche," v. 4; see also "Cántico Espiritual," vv. 6, 17–18.

[70] Barnstone, *The Poetics of Ecstasy*, 183.

[71] On Juan and the Bible, see Félix Garcia, "San Juan de la Cruz y
la Biblia," *Revista de Espiritualidad* 1 (1941–1942): 372–388; Alberto

to erotic language for metaphors about knowledge of and union with God, Juan finds himself in good company among many other mystics and theologians of his time.[72]

Where God is not known, nothing can be known.[73] Human persons, purged by divine fire "stand above" sensual distractions and detached from all false notions of God, are set free to love and know God.[74] But standing above sensuality does not mean disparaging bodily and sensorial expressions, including the experience of human sexuality. As Ruth Burrows cautions, we must be careful to interpret what may be perceived as disparaging statements regarding the body and its senses, for "we nearly always find an amending sentence somewhere or other by which we can interpret his seemingly inhuman injunction in a more balanced way."[75] As sensual creatures, "It is only in and through the full appropriation of the cataphatic moment . . . that is, by immersion in the beauty of the universe—that we can dialectically attain the negation of representations necessary for discovering that God is always more than we can conceive."[76] Or, as Juan bemoans, in what attracts us we are left like children babbling that God is "*un no sé qué*."[77]

Colunga, "San Juan de la Cruz intérprete de la Sagrada Escritura," *La Ciencia Tomista* 63 (1942): 257–276; Augustine Mulloor, "St. John of the Cross and the Sacred Scripture," *Living Word* 98 (1992): 443–451.

[72] Barnstone, *The Poetics of Ecstasy*, 182–183.

[73] CE, 26.13.

[74] CE, 25.11.

[75] Burrows, *Ascent to Love*, 94.

[76] Michael Bernard Kelly, *Christian Mysticism's Queer Flame: Spirituality in the Lives of Contemporary Gay Men* (New York: Routledge, 2019), 23; see also idem, *Seduced by Grace: Contemporary Spirituality, Gay Experience, and Christian Faith* (Melbourne: Clouds of Magellan, 2007).

[77] "*Y todos cuantos vagan, De ti me van mil gracias refiriendo, Y todos más me llagan, Y déjame muriendo, Un no sé qué que quedan balbuciendo.*" "The Spiritual Canticle," v. 7.

On Naming God as *un no sé qué*

The most fitting way to name God sanjuanistamente is to say that
God is "*un no sé qué*" (God is an "I know not what").[78] As a Christian mystic and theologian, Juan reflects a long-held tradition that
God's simple and immaterial nature demands that we let go of
visions, visible forms, figures, and "any particular knowledge and
unmodified boundaries associated with form, species, or image."[79]
In his poem "*Glosa a lo divino*," Juan uses the expression *un no sé
qué* at the end of each of its nine verses.[80] He affirms on the beauty
of God's creation and yet also invites us to set aside the beautiful
and pleasurable things encountered within the world.[81] "For all
the beauty in the world," Juan affirms in this poem, "I will not

---

[78] Juan uses the expression "*un no sé qué*" in a number of his writings
in ways that describe a kind of mystical sensing, feeling, intuition that
occurs when we face the mystery of God: "I do not think that those that
have not experienced this [mystical knowledge] will understand it well. But
since the soul that has experienced sees that it is unable to understand that
which it deeply feels, the soul calls it "*un no sé qué*." See the poem "Cantico
Espiritual," v. 7. In CE, 7, 9 Juan comments on this verse noting how the
expression *un no sé qué* refers to something felt but unexpressed, known but
not yet discovered, a sublime vestige of God awaiting investigation, a lofty
understanding of who God is that cannot be put into words ("*un altísimo
entender de Dios que no se sabe decir, que por eso lo llama no sé qué.*").

[79] S, 2.16, 7.

[80] "*Glossa a lo divino*," vv. 1–9.

[81] With respect to the prevalence of the attribute of beauty and
Juan's apophatic theology, A. N. Williams puts the question this way: "If
the created order should not detain our attention and therefore provides
no legitimate analogy in its own loveliness, how are we to envisage divine
beauty?" Williams goes on to respond that "Juan's apparently disparaging
comments about created things always stand in the context of the soul's
journey towards union: they are not judgments about the inherent value
of creatures, but solely about the usefulness of such things for a particular
end." See A. N. Williams, "The Doctrine of God in San Juan de la Cruz,"
Modern Theology 30, no. 4 (2014): 511.

surrender myself, but only for 'an I know not what' that may come to us by chance."[82] This reflects Juan's concern to guard against various forms of idolatry.

Human expressions that mediate the divine are constructions that fall short of God's mystery, and that may even betray it. Sexist, heterosexist, and racist ways of speaking about God are examples of the oppressive social constructs that have shaped God-talk. Such theologies both misrepresent God and impose harmful exclusionary practices that claim to deny how particular persons have access to God. Juan's reference to God as *"un no sé qué"* can help inoculate us against falling into that trap. While Juan's mysticism opens the door to encounter and name the mystery of God from the standpoints of many different human experiences, it also cautions us against turning any of these experiences into an idol.

Although we can know and name God in various ways, God cannot be confined to any of them. Juan invites us to consider that all naming of God should also involve un-naming. This alone is the surest way to prevent us from creating our golden calves. Ultimately, the main reason for which Juan proposes that God be named as *un no sé qué* is that God cannot be fully grasped by the human mind. At best we can sense God's presence, but God remains conceptually inaccessible, beyond all knowing and naming. A. N. Williams notes,

> The point here is not, however, that God is per se incomprehensible. The Spanish is even clearer in this respect than the English translation: *Dios "excede al entendimiento, y así es incomprehensible e inaccesible al entendimiento"*; the repetition the Carmelite translators avoided by rendering the second *entendimiento* as "it" Juan does not shrink

---

[82] See *"Glosa a lo Divino, del mismo autor,"* introduction and nine stanzas. See also Llama, 3.52.

from, thereby making clear that God is incomprehensible to the (human) understanding, rather than incomprehensible *in se*.[83]

Of course, even though God is a triune mystery, a God who *is* beyond all names, this does not mean that we are left with no recourse other than silence. At the most basic level, the Incarnation grounds all our efforts to relate human experiences to divine life and name in human ways the mystery of God. Juan follows this incarnational principle. His poems and prose offer rich names and metaphors that prompt and stretch our theological imagination with respect to envisioning the triune mystery of God.

"Living Flame of Love" and its commentary offer a way to think about the trinitarian mystery of God. Juan turns to metaphors of attraction, courtship, and carnal knowledge to evoke this mystery. Juan identifies the Father as God's "gentle hand"; the Son as God's "delicate touch;" and the Spirit as God's "sweet cautery."[84] In his commentary, Juan expands on each of these names and ascribes distinct functions to each of the divine persons. To the Father, he attributes the human transformation that pays all human "debt"; to the Son, the "taste of eternity"; and to the Spirit, the grace-filled capacity "to wound" us.[85] In thus naming the triune

---

[83] Williams, "The Doctrine of God," 509. Emphasis in original. See Llama, 3.48. On the omission of the repetition that makes the point about the limitations to knowing God being on the side of humans and not on the idea that God is incomprehensible see, for instance, *The Collected Works of John of the Cross*, and the translation of Llama, 3.48 as: "The reason is that God transcends the intellect and is incomprehensible to it." Emphasis added.

[84] "Llama," v. 2, and Llama, 2.1.

[85] Llama, 2.1. Juan uses the imagery of "wounds" across his corpus of works. See especially CE, 7, and Llama, 1.6–26. For a helpful discussion of this image, see Mary Frohlich, "'O Sweet Cautery': John of the Cross and the Healing of the Natural World," *Horizons* 43, no. 2 (2016): esp. 321–328, doi:10.1017/hor.2016.63.

mystery of God, Juan reflects the incarnational, healing, and forgiving nature of God.

Juan appeals to the image of God as light, arguing that God is "for the soul many lamps that distinctively offer warmth and light, and from which the soul attains knowledge and love of God."[86] In a way that bridges the apophatic and cataphatic elements of his theology, he speaks of this light as a dazzling ray of darkness that purifies and enables contemplation, and union with God.[87] Linking this metaphor of light with the experience of love and sexuality, he offers the central metaphor—the living flame—associated with divine and human love, and in particular with the Holy Spirit as God's living flame of love.[88]

The metaphorical connections between fire and human transformation also run throughout Juan's writings. We find frequent appeal to logs on fire as his way to describe the journey that leads to the union and the enkindling of love between divine and human persons that fuses and transforms each of them into the other.[89]

---

[86] Llama, 3.3.

[87] S, 2.8, 6; N, 2, 5 3; CE, 14, 15.16; Llama, 3.49.

[88] The question has been raised as to whether Juan understands love as the proper name of the Holy Spirit or of the divine essence itself and thereby shared in common with the three divine persons. George Tavard argues that "for John of the Cross, love is first of all neither a relation between Persons nor a person; it is the very essence of the Godhead, the *ousia* of the Three Persons. In essence God is lover, beloved, and love, in such a way that love is not distinct from beloved, lover from love, love from beloved." That said, Tavard goes on to admit that Juan does fall back on a more classical understanding that links love, or to be more theologically concise, divine personal love with the Holy Spirit. Is love only an "appropriation" of the essential love common to all three? Is it as in Thomas associated with the notion that for God to love "is no other than to 'spirate' love?" The question is unresolved, especially given the prevalent understanding in Juan's writings of the Spirit as God's living flame of love. See Tavard, *Poetry and Contemplation*, 138–139.

[89] Juan extensively comments on the image of a log on fire, comparing

Like logs that catch fire to become fire, humans too "catch" God to become Godlike.[90] Describing the transformative power of this divine fire of love and using spousal imagery, Juan writes:

> This flame of love is the spirit of his spouse, which is the Holy Spirit. The soul already senses this presence not only as a fire that transforms and consummates in delicate love, but as a fire that in addition to this, burns in the soul as I have expressed. And this flame, every time it inflames, bathes the soul in glory and refreshes the soul in the likeness of divine life.[91]

Juan's metaphors and names invite us to interrogate conventional ways of naming the divine within Christian traditions. His mystical theology remains relevant because he refuses to allow God to be restricted to any image, experience, category, or name. His mysticism queers conventional patterns of God-talk. For example, Juan has no difficulty portraying Christ as his lover, as his male spouse, and as his bridegroom.[92] Such gender-fluid language might be surprising to some, given that we are speaking about a sixteenth-century Iberian mystic. Although the male spousal imagery Juan uses retains a sexist identification of God, it breaks from binary and heteronormative understandings of relating divine and human persons. Juan describes his relationship to Christ in what we would understand today as gender-fluid ways. For example, his soul often performs as female and as the spouse of Christ.[93] Although his

---

the fire to God and the flaming logs to souls. See Llama, 1.1–36, especially Llama, 1.3; 1.19, 1.23, and 2.9.

[90] On the theme of catching God as prey, see Juan's poem "Tras de un Amoroso Lance."

[91] Llama, 1.3.

[92] See the poems "Cantico Espiritual," vv. 17, 27, 35; "Noche Oscura," v. 5; *Romances*, 1, 4.

[93] See the poem "Noche Oscura," vv. 5, 6.

writings reflect the culturally constructed gender stereotypes of his time vis-à-vis spousal relationships between men and women, they also make available the possibility of reading spousal imagery in more inclusive ways.

That said, although applying our contemporary consciousness with respect to issues of sexism would be anachronistic, Juan's theological metaphors do bear a certain degree of sexism by depicting the amatory relationship between divine and human persons through the experience of a male mystic passionately in love with Christ depicted as his male spouse. Interestingly, though, his writings also offer a fluid understanding of divine and human persons that can be used to challenge sexist and heterosexist understandings of the mystery of God.

Last, the metaphors and analogies that Juan draws are not exclusively male, nor do these metaphors meet the typical stereotypes associated with masculinity. He employs affectionate familiar terms to refer to God, often using the *tu* pronoun in Spanish. Among other familial metaphors, he depicts God as a nursing mother in his commentary on "Dark Night of the Soul."

It should be known, then, that God's Spirit raises and caresses the soul, after it has been resolutely converted to God's service, like a loving mother (*amorosa madre*) who warms her child with the heat of her bosom, nurses the child with good milk and tender food, and carries and caresses the child in her arms. But as the child grows older, the mother withholds her gift, her tender love (*tierno amor*); she rubs bitter aloes on her sweet breast and sets the child down from her arms, letting it walk on its own feet so that the child may put aside the habits of childhood and grow accustomed to greater and more important things (*cosas más grandes y substanciales*). The grace of God acts just as a loving mother by re-engendering in the soul

new enthusiasm and fervor in the service of God. With no
effort on the soul's part, this grace causes it to taste sweet
and delectable milk and to experience intense satisfaction
in the performance of spiritual exercises, because God is
offering the breast of God's tender love to the soul, just as
if it were a delicate child.[94]

In terms that portray the divine persons in a more egalitarian way,
he affectionately refers to Christ as our brother, arguing in the
image of familial love for the equality of human and divine persons
and their relationships with one another.[95]

The *un no sé qué* God Is Self-Communicating Love

The mystical journey that leads to union with God enables the true
self to emerge from the dark night into the dawn of day, and also
prepares the self to know and name, albeit imperfectly, the ineffable
mystery Juan calls "*un no sé qué.*" Stripped away from all that is not
God, human persons can truly encounter God. Or, as Juan would
say by appealing to his *todo-nada* dialectic (everything/nothing),
we strip ourselves of everything that is not God to discover God,
and everyone and everything in God.[96] The process of purification
and illumination that transforms the will and the mind has as its
central purpose to push us beyond familiar notions of where God
is found, how God is known, and how God is named.

The one whom Juan caressed, whose head he cradled upon his
flowering chest, the one he knew by savoring so well is known by
way of love. Juan came to know God, as lovers come to know each
other. Inflamed by God's self-communicative love, Juan rejoiced in

---

[94] N, 1.1, 2.
[95] CE, 24.5.
[96] See McGinn, *Mysticism in the Golden Age of Spain*, 267–269.

the night that brought him to consummate the divine love that he so deeply desired.[97] God's love, Juan never ceases to affirm, both binds divine and human persons, and transforms each into the other, just as lovers are transformed in sexual love and embodied communion. This transformation, this divinization, is the work of the triune God.

---

[97] "Noche Oscura," vv. 1, 3, 5.

3

God's Self-Communication

¡Oh cauterio suave!
¡Oh regalada llaga!
¡Oh mano blanda! ¡Oh toque delicado,
que a vida eterna sabe,
y toda deuda paga!
Matando, muerte en vida la has trocado.[1]

In contemporary Catholic theology, the understanding of grace as God's self-communication is most often connected with the work of Karl Rahner. He maintains that God's self-communication consists in that God the Son became incarnate and thereby fully human, entering our human experiences and assuming them as God's own.[2] Creation, and in particular the created humanity of Christ, is not God's afterthought but the expression of God's self-communication.[3] As such, human persons in their lived experiences become the addressees of God's self-communication. Rahner goes on to elaborate that in human persons God has created "a spiri-

---

[1] ¡O delicate cautery! O graced filled wound! O gentle hand! O delicate touch that tastes of eternal life and repays all my debt! Killing, you turn my death into life." "¡O Llama de Amor Viva!" v. 2.

[2] Karl Rahner, *The Trinity* (New York: Crossroad, 1997), 88–89.

[3] Rahner, *The Trinity*, 89.

tual-personal being, the only one who possesses the 'obediential potency' for reception of such self-communication."[4]

That God "becomes an intrinsic principle in human self-realization and not merely an asymptotic goal is solely due to God's gratuitous, free decision."[5] This gratuitous self-communication carries enormous implications for how we might read human experiences of sexuality *a lo divino*. While Juan's theological focus is on the desire to consummate union with God, in sexual union Juan finds an analogue for God's self-communication. For Juan, self-communitive love is at the heart of both divine and human forms of communication. And as his theology of mystical union suggests, sexual love can be understood, *mutatis mutandis*, as an outward expression of the triune mystery of God.

The "central theme of trinitarian theology," writes Catherine M. LaCugna, "is the relationship between the pattern of salvation history (*oikonomia*) and the eternal being of God (*theologia*)."[6] The contemporary revival of trinitarian theology rests on the fundamental insight that God is self-communicating love. "God by nature is self-expressive, God seeks to reveal and give Godself, God seeks to be united with other persons."[7] Because God is by nature self-expressive love, the economy of salvation becomes a window to contemplate and reflect upon the divine nature. This is the basis for Rahner's groundbreaking argument that the "economic Trinity is the immanent Trinity" (and vice versa).[8]

Reading Juan in the twenty-first century, in light of the trinitarian insights of Rahner and LaCugna, I propose that

---

[4] Rahner, *The Trinity*, 90.

[5] Stephen Duffy, *The Dynamics of Grace: Perspectives in Theological Anthropology* (Collegeville, MN: Liturgical Press, 1993), 312.

[6] Catherine M. LaCugna, *God for Us: The Trinity & Christian Life* (New York: HarperCollins, 1991), 230.

[7] LaCugna, *God for Us*, 230.

[8] Rahner, *The Trinity*, 38–45.

"To-Be" God, conceived sanjuanistamente, is to-be self-communicating love.[9] As A. N. Williams observes, "The whole of Juan's theology is founded on the doctrine of God, and more specifically, on the notion of divine communicability."[10] Juan de la Cruz's mystical theology, articulated especially through his poetry, turns our attention away from theological abstractions and toward a triune mystery that is shared so that we might partake in divine life. In Rahnerian terms, "The Trinity is not for us a reality which can only be expressed as a doctrine" but a mystery "bestowed upon us."[11]

God's capacity and desire for self-communication fulfills and perfects our desire to receive that communication.[12] But as Williams points out, "That which is given to humanity is never possessed, but this very non-possession tenders and sustains the dynamic and living relation between donor and recipient."[13] This personal relationship between God as donor and the human person as recipient is the key that unlocks Juan's mystical trinitarian theology. The loving relationship that God initiates with human persons enables them to taste, delight, and feast in divine life.[14] Here, Juan captures the heart of trinitarian theology, namely, that God chooses to act on our behalf in creation, revelation, and salva-

---

[9] On Juan's concept of the trinitarian indwelling of the Trinity, see Roberto Moretti, "Al vertice dell'esperienza trinitaria. Riflessioni sulla 'Fiamma viva d'amore' di San Giovanni della Croce," *Rivista di vita spirituale* 39 (1985): 172–185.

[10] A. N. Williams, "The Doctrine of God in San Juan de la Cruz," *Modern Theology* 30, no. 4 (2014): 502–503.

[11] Rahner, *The Trinity*, 39.

[12] Williams, "The Doctrine of God in San Juan de la Cruz," 502.

[13] Williams, "The Doctrine of God in San Juan de la Cruz," 503.

[14] Note the words that Juan uses to describe God's self-communication: *"que a vida eterna sabe," "Matando, muerte en vida la has trocado"* ("¡O Llama de Amor Viva!" v. 2.

tion.[15] To do so entails highlighting the amatory nature of God's self-communication, its recipients, and its effects.

God's Self-Communication
Conceived Sanjuanistamente

In Juan's trinitarian cartography, each of the divine persons situates for us distinctly the self-communication of God. The gentle hand, *mano blanda*, Juan associates with the Father who offers the gift of paying the human debt that enables human transformation. The Son offers the gift of divine delicate touch, *el toque delicado*, that makes union with God possible. And in the Holy Spirit, this union with God can be consummated through the consuming and cauterizing fire of divine love, the cautery, *el cauterio suave*. Although each person carries out a specific role in this divine labor of love, Juan echoes conventional theological wisdom in affirming the interdependence of the divine persons, and because they all work as one, everything is attributed to one and to all, *"porque todos ellos obran en uno, y así, todo lo atribuye a uno, y todo a todos."*[16]

In his poems and commentaries, Juan often uses the metaphor of fire to convey the notion of God as self-communicating love. "The Holy Trinity," Juan writes, "inhabits such a soul that enflames it in two ways—through the habitual union of love like glowing embers, and through the union of active burning love like flames shooting from embers."[17] It is the Holy Spirit that Juan characterizes specifi-

---

[15] See Walter Kasper, who observes that "the Christian's concern is not with God in himself but with God-for-us, the God of Jesus Christ, who is a God of human beings (Heb. 11.16)." See Walter Kasper, *The God of Jesus Christ* (New York: Crossroad, 1989), 158.

[16] Llama, 2.1. All the material in this paragraph is from Juan's commentary on the quoted stanza from the poem "Llama" that opens this chapter of *Queer God de Amor.*

[17] For a discussion on Juan's anthropology, see Bernard McGinn,

cally as God's living flame of love. The Spirit is the divine matchmaker who leads us into an intimate union with Christ, our beloved spouse. In this divine flame, we become sharers in divine life and love.

The shift in emphasis from considering grace as an entity to understanding grace as God's personal self-communication is a subject of contemporary theological reflections.[18] "Today," writes Roger Haight, S.J, "more and more Catholic theologians are abandoning the Scholastic language of grace . . . calling for a theology of grace in personalist categories."[19] As a sixteenth-century voice, Juan might be said to anticipate this direction in his talk of the intimate and personal indwelling of divine life in human persons made possible by God's living flame of love. His use of sensual and loving metaphors in his poetic imagery referencing the inner life of the Trinity, the incarnation (and hypostatic union), and the relationship between God and humanity highlights dimensions of divine self-disclosure.[20] We can summarize Juan's approach to God's self-communication in the following way: God sends the Word, Jesus Christ, to become incarnate, thereby entering into intimate union with us.[21] God charges the Spirit, the divine flame of love, with the work of human transformation. The Spirit enkindles the divine

Mysticism in the Golden Age of Spain (1500–1650), vol. 6, part 2 of *The Presence of God: A History of Western Christian Mysticism* (New York: Crossroad, 2017), 253–261, and Kieran Kavanaugh, O.C.D, ed., *John of the Cross: Selected Writings* (New York: Paulist Press, 1987), 303.

[18] On the contemporary Catholic developments for the doctrine of grace, see Karl Rahner, "Some Implications of the Scholastic Concept of Uncreated Grace," in *Theological Investigations* I (New York: Crossroad, 1974), 319–346, and Rahner, "Nature and Grace," in *Theological Investigations*, IV (New York: Crossroad, 1982), 165–188. See also Duffy, *The Dynamics of Grace*, esp. 261–343.

[19] Roger Haight, SJ, *The Experience and Language of Grace* (Mahwah, NJ: Paulist Press, 1979), 96.

[20] See *Romances*, 1–9.

[21] See *Romances*, 3.

seduction and enables the amorous relationship and union with Christ, our beloved spouse.[22]

Divine love does not remain locked in an intra-divine and restrictive interpersonal relationship. For Juan divine love necessarily pours out in pursuit of human love. In his mystical theology love "almost always expresses a relation between God and creation, rather than expressing an intra-divine relationality."[23] Juan's God is undoubtedly a relational God, but essential to expressing this relationality is its communicability "outside" of God. Trinitarian theology in the past has devoted too much attention reflecting on the "immanent" life of God, in efforts to preserve divine freedom and affirm the legitimate distinctions between divine and human life. LaCugna explains, "A great deal of confusion is generated by the fact that 'immanent Trinity' is often used imprecisely, either to mean the interior life of God, or as a synonym for the divine essence."[24] Drawing on Rahner, she continues, "An immanent trinitarian theology, in other words, cannot be an analysis of what is 'inside' God, but a way of thinking and speaking about the structure or pattern of God's self-expression in salvation history."[25] Juan's mystical theology, while preserving legitimate distinctions between divine Lover and beloved human persons, underscores the self-communicating nature of the former for the sake of transforming and uniting with the latter.

Juan's mystical theology highlights God's eternal being, but his focus is on God's triune self-communication. Trinitarian life, to paraphrase Juan, is about God's desire to unite with human persons. God communicates Godself in love so that we might be

---

[22] See Willis Barnstone, "Mystico-Erotic Love 'O Living Flame of Love,'" *Revista Hispánica Moderna,* 37, no. 4 (1972–1973): 253–261.

[23] Williams, "The Doctrine of God," 520.

[24] LaCugna, *God for Us,* 224.

[25] LaCugna, *God for Us,* 225.

given, as Juan puts it, a "taste" of eternity.[26] God reaches us through divine "touch" resonating with contemporary Christian claims that "the life of God is not something that belongs to God alone. Trinitarian *life is also our life.*"[27]

Juan's trinitarian theology is most evident in his *Romances*, nine poems composed during his nine months of imprisonment in 1578.[28] Across these romances, or ballads, Juan eloquently describes the interdependence of divine persons that characterizes divine life. Reflecting on the Prologue of John's Gospel, Juan describes the Word as eternally "dwelling" in God, "conceived" from the "substance" of God, and full of the Father's glory.[29] Infinite love unites the divine persons in an ineffable "knot."[30]

> *As the beloved in the lover*
> *one in the other resides,*
> *and that love which unites them*
> *is one with them,*
> *with the one and the other*
> *in equality and excellence*
> *three persons, and one beloved*
> *among the three.*
> *And one love among them all.*[31]

---

[26] "Living Flame of Love," v. 2.

[27] LaCugna, *God for Us*, 228. Emphasis in original.

[28] "John's commentaries are not doctrinal treatises. Often overlooked, the 'Nine Romances,' poems he composed while in prison in imitation of contemporary popular ballads, are perhaps the best source for the doctrine that underlies his teaching." See McGinn, *Mysticism in the Golden Age of Spain*, 246.

[29] *Romances*, 1: "*El verbo se llama Hijo, / que del principio nacía; / hale siempre concebido / y siempre le concebía; / dale siempre su sustancia, / y siempre se la tenía.*"

[30] *Romances*, 1: "*Este ser es cada una, / y éste solo la unía / en un inefable nudo / que decir no se sabía; / por lo cual era infinito / el amor que las unía.*"

[31] *Romances*, 1.

Juan uses the imagery of spousal union to describe how divine and human life come together in Christ. Not only is the Son a gift to humanity, but humanity is also offered as a spousal gift to the Son.[32] The whole of creation, including humanity in a special way, becomes the "palace" for the self-communication and expression of divine love.[33] In this way, Jesus Christ, as God's self-communication, creates an intimate space for all human persons to unite with God and become God's self-expression.[34] In other words, the divine spouse enables human persons to share the likeness of God because perfect love calls for similarity between lover and beloved.[35] The Father tells the Son, "Your spouse was made in your own image and in that which is like you, she was well-suited."[36] Although the incarnation is the work of the Triune God, it is accomplished in the Word in whom the Trinity is clothed with flesh and lived incarnate in the womb of Mary.[37] In taking on the flesh of the bride in the incarnation the Son also takes her weariness and labors, the sufferings that burden her, and a willingness to sacrifice his own life that she might live.[38]

While these poems clearly recognize the intra-divine communication among the divine persons, Juan's mysticism focuses on the self-communication of God to humanity. As the Father, Son, and Spirit live in one another, so too will the bride. Taken into God,

---

[32] *Romances*, 3: "*Una esposa que te ame, mi Hijo darte quería...*"

[33] *Romances*, 4: "*el mundo criado había / palacio para la esposa hecho en gran sabiduría...*"

[34] *Romances*, 7.

[35] *Romances*, 7: "*En los amores perfectos esta ley se requería: que se haga semejante el amante a quien quería.*"

[36] *Romances*, 7: "*Ya ves, Hijo que a tu esposa / a tu imagen hecho había, / y en lo que a ti se parece / contigo bien convenía; / pero difiore en la carne / que en tu simple ser no había.*"

[37] *Romances*, 8: "*en la cual la Trinidad / de carne al Verbo vestía; / Y aunque tres hacen la obra, / en el uno se hacía....*"

[38] *Romances*, 7.

she would share in the divine life.[39] This self-communication is the ground for the love that binds human and divine life as well as human persons to one another. Looking at the poems "The Dark Night" and "Romance 1," Colin Thompson identifies Juan's analogous use of amatory and spousal imagery to elucidate these relationships.

> San Juan's ballads deal with the doctrines of the Trinity, Creation, and Incarnation. Yet he chooses to present them not in dogmatic or philosophical terms but in terms of *Heilsgeschichte*, the history of salvation, and in them he privileges the symbol of conjugal love, central to his *lira* poems, above all others. . . . *The bond this creates with the liras is never clearer than in the first ballad, where the relationship of Father to Son, "como amado en el amante" (line 21), "as beloved in the lover", is matched in the fifth verse of the "Noche", "amada en el amado transformada", "lover transformed in the beloved". The "Noche", however, represents the union of the human lover with the divine Beloved, while the ballad marks the union of the divine Persons of Father and Son as simile, since they cannot be lovers in any literal sense.* The ballads reveal how the union of love between the divine Persons creates for the Son a bride in his image and likeness, "ymagen" and "semejança" leads him to seek her out in her tribulations, become one with her in human flesh . . . and raise her to divinity.[40]

To speak of God's self-communication sanjuanistamente is to describe the divine Lover courting a human spouse. This divine

---

[39] *Romance*s, 4: "*que, como el Padre y el Hijo, / y el que de ellos procedía / el uno vive en el otro, / así la esposa sería, / que, dentro de Dios absorta, / vida de Dios viviría.*"

[40] Colin P. Thompson, *St. John of the Cross: Songs in the Night* (Washington, DC: Catholic University of America, 2003), 57. Emphasis added.

courtship manifests itself in various forms and impacts distinct aspects of the communally and the socially informed human soul.[41] Juan tells us that our desire to unite with our divine spouse becomes so irresistible that we are led to proclaim: "Be done, if you will, and tear through the veil of this sweet encounter."[42] That is to say, "Consummate perfectly with me the spiritual marriage with your beatific vision."[43] For Juan, this represents the moment of intense joy and celebration that results from reaching the summit of God's self-communication.[44] Here the beloved is so intimately close to, and so inflamed by, God's love that they enjoy a foretaste of heaven, "transformed into the flame of love, in which the Father, the Son, and the Holy Spirit are communicated."[45]

The Recipient of God's Self-Communication

Juan's theological anthropology is complex and his preference for poetry adds nuance. My aim is to challenge overly spiritualized, disembodied, and sanitized interpretations of Juan's presentation of the mystical subject. His apophatic focus, expressed in his call to negate the senses and human experiences, can lead to interpretations of Juan's work that disparage or dismiss the incarnate dimension of being *capax Dei*. Juan's theologizing is not only about the "dark night," or setting aside unnecessary distractions that take us away from God. He is also a cataphatic theologian who emphasizes the goodness of created realities and the presence

---

[41] CE, 11. 2–5.

[42] "Llama," v. 1

[43] Llama, 1.27.

[44] Llama 2.36: "*En este estado de vida tan perfecta siempre el alma anda interior y exteriormente como de fiesta, y trae con gran frecuencia en el paladar de su espíritu un júbilo de Dios grande, como un cantar nuevo, siempre nuevo envuelto en alegría y amor en conocimiento de su feliz estado.*"

[45] Llama, 1.6.

of God in human experiences. Few places in his writings make this point clearer than his poem and commentary on the living flame of God's love.

Love binds the divine giver to the human recipient. Juan admits that sometimes we experience more knowledge of God than love and at other times more love than knowledge. He proposes that God can "communicate to one faculty and not to the other, thereby inflaming the will with the touch of God's love, even if the intellect fails to understand, just like a person can be heated by fire without seeing it."[46]

The human reality that constitutes the recipient of God's self-communication includes the senses and appetites. It also includes a more spiritual side composed of the faculties of memory, understanding, and will.[47] Central to our humanity is what Juan calls the substance, center, or core of our being where God's self-communication occurs most intensely.[48] This is the place where God's triune life becomes most palpable.[49] This core integrates the spiritual faculties and physical senses so that the human person can receive God's self-communication holistically.[50] Edward Howells writes:

> The final purpose of union, for John, is not to attain an "unfleshed," heavenly state but to enter fully into incarnate life. He says that our union here "is not as essential

---

[46] Llama, 3.49.

[47] For a discussion on Juan's anthropology, see McGinn, *Mysticism in the Golden Age of Spain*, 34–37.

[48] See Edward Howells, *John of the Cross and Teresa of Avila: Mystical Knowing and Selfhood* (New York: Crossroad, 2002), 55.

[49] Llama, 1.9–13, 2.34–36. Please note that "place" does not imply physically localizing the self-communication of God spatially because the soul and this core of human personality cannot be localized, and, as Juan suggests, it is distinctly expressed in the spiritual-embodied activities of human persons.

[50] See Howells, *John of the Cross and Teresa of Avila*, 55–59.

and perfect as in the next life," and the "sensitive veil" of the flesh remains between our present state and glory. Union gives us a taste and a longing for heaven. Yet God has fortified our sensory flesh to enable us to enter into the "consummation" of union and to be of service in the world. John sees in Christ, incarnate and resurrected, the full possibility for human flesh where the body becomes the perfect *expression* of the clarified spirit.[51]

Juan's position concerning God's role in fortifying and perfecting the flesh, raises a key issue in Catholic theological anthropology, namely, the relation between nature and grace.[52] Juan's theology of grace highlights the fortifying presence of grace that enables the human ascent from, through, and in divine love. All human flesh is in need of this fortification. All expressions of human love need to be inflamed by God's living flame of love so that they can participate in divine life. For Juan, it seems axiomatic to affirm that the Incarnation would have happened, even if there had been no sin, because God is self-communicating love. That love binds divine persons and serves as the link between divine and human persons and human persons to one another.[53]

In his commentary on "Living Flame of Love," Juan discusses the experience of transverberation. To describe mystical communion Juan uses an erotic metaphor in which a seraph uses a dart to pierce the human soul. The cauterizing dart symbolizes God's

---

[51] Howells, *John of the Cross and Teresa of Avila*, 59. Emphasis in original.

[52] On this relationship, see Karl Rahner's classical essay, "Nature and Grace," 165–188.

[53] See, for instance, *Romances*, 3 and 4. In these stanzas Juan basically echoes Bonaventure's principle of creation being the expression of God's self-diffusive love. He interprets God's creation for the purposes of establishing a partner, spouse for Christ.

self-communication.[54] The in-bodied disruptions and impetuous motions of the recipient of these actions signal the effects of this self-communication.[55] The more God's living flame of love penetrates us as recipients of grace, the more Godlike we become, to the point when we ourselves become God's living flames of love.[56] Juan writes,

> It will come to pass that when the soul is inflamed in the love of God . . . the soul will feel assailed by a seraphim's arrow, through a dart so inflamed by the fire of love, that it pierces what is already an enkindled soul, as an ember penetrates, or more precisely, as a flame increasingly

---

[54] *Romances*, 1, and "The Dark Night," v. 5. By far the best known image of transverberation is Gian Lorenzo Bernini's 1652 marble sculpture depicting Saint Teresa of Ávila in ecstasy, located in the Cornaro Chapel of the Church of Santa Maria della Vittoria in Rome.

[55] Note Juan's use of the concept of "trabucamiento" (transformative, disruptive) and "mocion" (fluidity, dynamism, motion) in describing the seraph's penetrating love: "*y entonces, al herir de este encendido dardo, siente la llaga del alma en deleite sobremanera, porque, demás de ser ella toda removida en gran suavidad al trabucamiento y moción impetuosa causada por aquel serafín, en que siente grande ardor y derretimiento de amor,*" Llama, 2.9. For a discussion of the etymology of the words "trabucamiento and his concept of "moción," see Rosario Domínguez, "La creación léxica en la prosa de San Juan de la Cruz: neologismos sustantivos y variantes," *Epos* 7 (1991): 183–214.

[56] "*en que se hace tal junta de las dos naturalezas y tal comunicación de la divina a la humana, que, no mudando alguna de ellas su ser, cada una parece Dios, aunque en esta vida no puede ser perfectamente . . .*" CE, 22, 5. Note two ways that Juan uses the metaphor of fire. Dicken writes that in the poem "the effect of the fire is to wound and cauterize the flesh. In the commentary, first the fire heats the wood and drives off its moisture and sap. Then as the wood becomes dry and hotter, the fire kindles it and unites with it and turns the wood itself to flame." See E. W. Trueman Dicken, *The Crucible of Love: A Study of the Mysticism of St. Teresa of Jesus and St. John of the Cross* (New York: Sheed and Ward, 1963), 465.

cauterizing the soul. And then, with this cauterization and piercing, the flame intensifies and ascends vehemently, like the fire in a furnace or oven intensifies when upon being stirred and poked to excite it. And then injured by this inflamed dart, the soul feels this wound with infinite delight. The soul is stirred into great sweetness from the seraphim's disruptive and impetuous motion. It feels intense heat as it melts away in love. The soul feels the delicate wound and the herb, which keenly tempered the iron, as though it were a living point in the substance of the spirit, as in the heart of a pierced soul.[57]

The Effects of God's Self-Communication

As this erotic metaphor of the seraphim's penetrating and transformative act suggests, the effects of God's self-communication are not merely spiritual. Grace transforms whole persons. This is evident in the "The Dark Night," for example, where in the transformation of lover and beloved, *amado y amada* are fused and transformed one into the other.[58] Juan's eloquent use of erotic metaphor invites us to discover in human sexual experience the embodied language that makes it possible to appreciate and to experience divine self-disclosure.

Just as a fire can intensify and spread over time, God's self-communication intensifies and permeates the entire spiritual-sensorial reality of human persons. In his commentary on "Living Flame of Love" Juan employs a metaphor of a log immersed in fire to explain this relationship. He writes:

It is sufficient to know that the very God who desires to enter within the soul through union and transformation of love is he who first assails and purges it with the light

---

[57] Llama, 2.9.
[58] "Noche," v. 5.

and heat of his divine flame, just as the fire that penetrates the log of wood is the same that first prepares it for this as I have stated before. Hence the very flame that is now gentle, since it has entered within the soul, is what was formerly oppressive, assailing it from without.[59]

Sexual union can bridge the distance between lovers, without erasing each of their distinct ways of being human, and enables them to share in the transformative power of love. Similarly, Juan urges that in mystical union, human persons share God's life, so that "the soul's understanding becomes God's understanding; its will, God's will; and its memory God's eternal memory; its delight, God's delight. And even though the substance of this soul is not the substance of God, because the soul cannot be changed substantially into God, it becomes God as a result of its participation, having been united to God and absorbed in God."[60] In other words, transformed in God's living flame of love, the human soul "becomes God from God through participation in God and in God's attributes."[61]

To conceive the effects of grace on the soul is also to consider the bodily exteriorization of grace. Setting aside distracting attachments and silencing the senses are Juan's preconditions to achieve mystical union with God. While it is beyond the scope of this book to elaborate further on this, it is clear that Juan understands that the effects of God's living flame are not simply spiritual in nature but can and do overflow into embodied manifestations. "Sometimes," writes Juan, "the unction of the Holy Spirit overflows in the body, and the entire sensorial substance, all the members, bones, and marrow rejoice, not lightly as is customary,

---

[59] Llama, 2.25.
[60] Llama, 2.34.
[61] Llama, 3.8.

but with great delight and glory, felt all the way to the extremities of our feet and hands."[62]

Affirming the possibility for God's self-communicating love to express itself through ordinary and embodied experiences cannot be overstated. If, as Juan may be taken to affirm, God is self-communicating love, then we must take seriously the ways in which human self-expressions, especially those associated with the articulation of love, including sexual love, mirror, participate in, and exteriorize God's triune love. For us to read human sexual experience *a lo divino*, as inspired by reflection on "Living Flame of Love," Juan's commentary, and the *Romances*, opens possibilities of understanding his appeal to human sexuality and the sexual subject not only as metaphors that describe divine love, but in a Catholic analogical sense, as expressions of the love of the triune God. Perhaps such a reading also invites deeper theological consideration of sexual union and other self-expressive and mutual acts of love.

On Divine and Human Self-Communicating Love

Juan's writings invite us to distinguish between God's self-communication and the creaturely communications about God that may stand in the way of reception.[63] The point of making such a distinction is to guard against idolatry. God's self-communication works to reorient and awaken us to receive God's loving touch. In turn, this reorientation, by transforming our spiritual faculties and bodily senses, makes it possible for us to participate in God's triune love.

Juan affirms that human persons possess an innate spiritual capacity for God. He ties this spiritual capacity specifically to the

---

[62] Llama, 2.22.

[63] See Ruth Burrows, *Ascent to Love: The Spiritual Teaching of St. John of the Cross* (Denville, NJ: Dimensions, 1987), 73.

faculties of memory, understanding, and will, which he calls the "deep caverns," *profundas cavernas*, within the soul.[64] He speaks of the thirst of the intellect "for the waters of God's wisdom;"[65] of the hunger of the will for "the perfection of love after which the soul aims;"[66] and of the yearning of memory to receive God.[67] The more human beings desire and search for their divine beloved, even more does God desire and search for them.[68] Juan is a Christian mystic shaped by an incarnational spirituality. We must avoid the temptation to spiritualize his theology at the expense of diluting the power of his rich, romantic, and sensual language to inspire imaginations in ways that help us contemplate the fullness of communion with the divine. The erotic language of his poetry opens the senses, heart, mind, and will to consummate our union with God, our lover, in this life, and in the one to come.

As human beings receive God's self-communication we enter more deeply into the world of our human experience and rediscover its true meaning in love. The fluidity with which Juan speaks of God in embodied language opens paths forward for contemporary theologies that take gender and sexuality seriously in order to reimagine God's self-communication in ways that interrupt limited theologies of grace.[69]

---

[64] Llama, 3.18.

[65] Llama, 3.19.

[66] Llama, 3.20.

[67] Llama, 3.21.

[68] Llama, 3.23, 3.28.

[69] For an example of a contemporary theology that takes gender seriously, see Elizabeth Johnson, *She Who Is: The Mystery of God in Feminist Theological Discourse* (New York: Crossroad, 1992), esp. 42–59.

4

ECSTASIS DIVINE AND HUMAN

¡Oh lámparas de fuego,
en cuyos resplandores las profundas
cavernas de sentido,
que estaba oscuro y ciego,
Con extraños primores
calor y luz dan junto a su Querido![1]

Trinitarian theology is constructed upon the pillars of person, relationship, and communion.[2] Catherine M. LaCugna observes, "The central presupposition of the Christian doctrine of God is the encounter between divine and human persons in the economy of redemption. Indeed, trinitarian theology is par excellence

---

[1] "O lamps of fire in whose splendors the deep caverns of the senses, once obscured and blind, now give forth, so rarely and exquisitely, both warmth and light to her (his) Beloved!" "Llama," v. 3.

2 See Catherine M. LaCugna, *God for Us: The Trinity and Christian Life* (New York: HarperCollins, 1991), 243–317; John Zizioulas, *Communion & Otherness* (New York: T&T Clark, 2006), 99–112, 155–177; Patricia A. Fox, *God as Communion: John Zizioulas, Elizabeth Johnson, and the Retrieval of the Symbol of the Triune God* (Collegeville, MN: Liturgical Press, 2010), 25–98. For a Thomistic philosophical exploration on a relational metaphysics see W. Norris Clarke, S.J., *The One and the Many: A Contemporary Thomistic Metaphysics* (Notre Dame, IN: University of Notre Dame Press, 2001).

a theology of relationship: God to us, we to God, we to each other."[3] Juan de la Cruz's trinitarian theology builds upon these pillars to express the mystical encounters that take place between divine and human persons. In portraying the movement of God as Lover to human persons, and their movement in return to unite with God, Juan reflects this relational and communal theological anthropology. This interpersonal dynamism that welcomes human persons into divine life is what characterizes the mystical experience of ecstasy.

Ecstasy entails a journey of personal relationship, transformation, and communion. "Whether the journey is seen as one that passes into the darkness of the unknowing that is knowing, or ends in the light of vision, both God and the human person go outside themselves so that each may become united to the other."[4] In the context of mystical experience, ecstasy mirrors "the intense pleasure of sexual union, in which the lover feels momentarily transported out of himself or herself in union with the beloved."[5] Human persons are ecstatic beings created in the image of God's self-expressive love, and so they must also be understood as sexual beings. LaCugna defines sexuality broadly as "the capacity for relationship, for ecstasis, and for self-transcendence," and so, "an icon of who God is."[6]

"Living Flame of Love" highlights the infinite possibilities we have as human persons to relate to God. As self-communicating love, God enflames and enlightens us to participate in divine life.[7]

---

[3] LaCugna, *God for Us*, 243.

[4] LaCugna, *God for Us*, 351.

[5] LaCugna, *God for Us*, 351.

[6] LaCugna, *God for Us*, 406–407.

[7] For example, see verse 3 that begins this chapter. Juan appeals to the metaphors of lamps of fire and deep caverns. He uses the metaphor of the lamps in reference to the divine attributes that God freely shares with human persons. The deep caverns represent the infinite human capacity for

God draws us out of ourselves so that we might become expressions of divine love. This self-expression of God, which enables our self-expression in God, transforms divine and human persons, "one into the other."[8] In addressing this theology of interpersonal ecstasis, the perichoresis that characterizes divine and human persons, the dynamic and fluid understandings of divine and human persons, and the amorous desire that propels them to relate and unite with one another deserves attention.

Making Room for Another

The trinitarian notion of perichoresis offers an appropriate way to begin discussion of Juan's theology of divine and human persons. The term has a long history in Christology and trinitarian theology. "The verb *perichorein* was introduced into christological language by Gregory of Nazianzen (d. ca. 389), the noun *perichoresis* by Maximus the Confessor (d. ca. 662). Both were extended into trinitarian language by an anonymous author known as Pseudo-Cyril (ca. 650) and popularized by John of Damascus (d. ca. 749)."[9] Within trinitarian theology, *perichoresis* is a concept that highlights the interdependence, coinherence, and co-indwelling of the divine persons. It refers primarily to the dynamic relationship in which the divine persons "make room" for one another but also to the manifold ways spouses "explore, discover, and fulfill their

---

God, primarily related to the spiritual faculties of memory, understanding and will. See Llama, 3.2; 3.17.

    8 "Noche Oscura," v. 5.

    9 Michael G. Lawler, "Perichoresis: New Theological Wine in an Old Theological Wineskin," *Horizons* 22, no. 1 (1995): 50. See also LaCugna, *God for Us*, 270–278; Emmanuel Durand, O.P., "Perichoresis: A Key Concept for Balancing Trinitarian Theology," in *Rethinking Trinitarian Theology: Disputed Questions and Contemporary Issues in Trinitarian Theology*, ed. Robert J. Wozniak and Giulio Maspero (New York: T&T Clark, 2012), 177–192.

individual and mutual possibilities" in relating and sexually uniting with one another.[10]

Several of Juan's writings address this lavish act of hospitality, which not only makes room for the divine persons but also makes room for humans. Consider Juan's *Romances*. These nine ballads reflect on how the triune life of God expresses itself in Christ and in all of creation.[11] The first Romance introduces the perichoretic movement that characterizes divine life, as the lover in the beloved, in which each resides in the other, "*Como amado en el amante, Uno en otro residía.*"[12] The eternal "making room" of the divine persons that enables them to intimately abide in one another is temporally expressed in the divine touch that leads to creation, Incarnation, and the transformation and union of human persons to God.

In Juan's *Romances* the Incarnation is addressed in terms of God's spousal union with humanity.[13] Juan begins this series of ballads by pondering the intra-divine relationship, affirming traditional Christian teaching regarding the equality, interdependence, and mutuality of the divine persons. He describes how the divine persons share one common essence, but distinctly express it as Father, Son, and Spirit. Love, according to Juan, binds the divine persons and constitutes divine life: "And therefore, was boundless, the love that united them. Because the three only have one love, as

---

[10] Lawler, "Perichoresis," 58.

[11] For instance, see *Romances, 1*: "*En el principio moraba / el Verbo, y en Dios vivía, / en quien su felicidad / infinita poseía.*" (In the beginning dwelled the Word, and in God the Word was living, in whom it found infinite happiness"); and *Romances* 4: "*Hágase, pues"—dijo el Padre—Que tu amor lo merecía. Y en este dicho que dijo, El mundo criado había.*" ["Let it be done," then, said the Father, for your love merited it. And in so saying it the world was created.]

[12] In *Romances, 1*.

[13] The Incarnation is explicitly addressed in *Romances* 7 and 8, the birth of the Son in 9. *Romances* 4 also contains spousal imagery regarding incarnation.

we say with respect to their essence. That the more love unites, the more love it creates."[14]

Juan parts ways with some earlier conceptions of the Trinity when it comes to his understanding of the nature of divine love and its expression in each of the divine persons. George Tavard observes that by equating the Lover and the Beloved,[15] "John of the Cross, whether consciously or not, departed from traditional Trinitarian theologies rooted in love, as that of St. Augustine in Book 8 of his treatise *On the Trinity*, or that of Richard of St. Victor (1104–73) in his book bearing the same title."[16]

According to Augustine, the Father is the one who loves, the Son is the one loved, and the Spirit serves as the bond of love between the Father and the Son (*amans, quod amatur, amor*). This has become the prominent model of Western trinitarian theologies.[17] Richard of St. Victor sees the Father as the Lover who loves the Son and the Spirit as the co-beloved of the Father and the Son. Juan's trinitarian Romance, argues Tavard, "follows neither of these models."[18] As Tavard points out, in these *Romances*, Juan's Beloved, is identified with the three divine persons, rather than with any one of them. The implication is that love not only constitutes the nature of God but is what binds each of the persons to one another. Tavard argues that here, Juan is taking his cue from the Johannine

---

[14] In *Romances*, 1, Juan writes: *"Por lo cual era infinito el amor que las unía, porque un solo amor tres tienen, que su esencia se decía; que el amor, cuanto mas uno, tanto más amor hacía."*

[15] Juan writes in reference to the divine persons: *"y un amor en todas ellas / y un amante las hacía, y el amante es el amado / en que cada cual vivía."* *Romances*, 1.

[16] George H. Tavard, *Poetry and Contemplation in St. John of the Cross* (Athens: Ohio University, 1988), 137.

[17] See Michel René Barnes, "Latin Trinitarian Theology," in *The Cambridge Companion to the Trinity*, ed. Peter C. Phan (Cambridge, UK: Cambridge University Press, 2011), 70–84.

[18] Tavard, *Poetry and Contemplation*, 138.

understanding that affirms that God is love (1 John 4:8, 16). This divine love is also the foundation for all human expressions of love. As the often-cited cliché among queer persons puts it, "love is love":

> For John of the Cross, love is first of all neither a relation between Persons nor a Person; it is the very essence of the Godhead, the *ousia* of the Three Persons. In essence God is lover, beloved, and love, in such a way that love is not distinct from beloved, lover from love, love from beloved.[19]

In the second of these *Romances*, Juan deepens his reflection on the intra-divine communication of the divine persons. This ballad sets up a dialogue between the Father and the Son to describe the intimate accompaniment and the delight of the Father who loves the Son and all persons and things through the Son.[20] The Father describes the Son as being light of his light, his wisdom, and image of his substance.[21] Above all, the Father tells the Son that love will cause God's self-gift to humanity. "My Son," the Father professes, "I will give myself / to the one who loves you / and I will love that one / with the same love I have for you, / because that one has loved / you whom I love so."[22]

The next three Romances address the relationship of the divine persons to creation. They echo the traditional Latin approach represented by Thomas Aquinas that understands the divine processions *ad intra* as the ground for the divine missions *ad extra*.[23] In these Romances, Juan begins to transition from

---

[19] Tavard, *Poetry and Contemplation*, 138.

[20] "*Nada me contenta, Hijo, / fuera de tu compañía.*" *Romances*, 2.

[21] "*Eres lumbre de mi lumbre, / eres mi sabiduría, / figura de substancia, / en quien bien me complacía.*" *Romances*, 2.

[22] "*Al que a ti te amare, Hijo, a mí mismo le daría.*" *Romances*, 2.

[23] On Aquinas's way of relating processions and missions see LaCugna, *God for Us*, 152–160.

intra-divine perichoresis to the notion that in Christ, God's life of mutual love reaches outward to make room for human persons and all of creation. Trinitarian life does not belong to God alone, but is intended to be shared through Christ, our beloved spouse.

The third Romance opens with the promise of the Father to give the Son a spouse who will love him in return and because of him will participate in the fullness of divine life, "share our company, and eat at our table." In the Son the bride shall see the greatness of the Father; in his arms she will exalt God's goodness.[24] In the fourth Romance Juan suggests that the work of creation is a preparation for the Incarnation. In arguing that God would be human, so humans could be God, he echoes Athanasius's classic affirmation: "He was made human so that he might be made God."[25] The Romance concludes describing the human participation in the eternal and divine perichoresis: "The one lives in the other, and so that is how it will be with the spouse, for taken into God, she will live the life of God."[26]

Romances 5 and 6 describe humanity's yearning for the advent of the bridegroom. Romances 7, 8, and 9 reflect on the Incarnation. Juan connects the life of God, the cross, and human salvation.[27] Of particular interest in these Romances is Juan's affirmation that in perfect love the beloved must be made like the lover: "For the

---

[24] "*Una esposa que te ame, mi Hijo darte quería / . . . Reclinarla he yo en mi brazo, / y en tu amor se abrasaría, / y con eterno deleite / tu bondad sublimaría.*" *Romances*, 3.

[25] "*porque en todo semejante / él a ellos se haría / y se vendría con ellos / y con ellos moraría / y que Dios sería hombre, / y que el hombre Dios sería.*" In *Romances*, 4. On Athanasius, see *De incarnatione* 54.3, Saint Athanasius, *On the Incarnation*, ed. John Behr (Yonkers, NY: St. Vladimir's Seminary Press, 2012).

[26] "*el uno vive en el otro, / así la esposa sería, / que, dentro de Dios absorta, / vida de Dios viviría.*" *Romances*, 4.

[27] "*Iré a buscar a mi esposa, / . . . y porque ella vida tenga, / yo por ella moriría . . .*" *Romances*, 7.

greater the likeness, the greater the delight."[28] The Son owes this flesh to the flesh of Mary, and "so he is called Son of God and of humanity."[29] Juan concludes the *Romances* with a reflection on the birth of Jesus, calling him the spouse who goes out from the bridal chamber to embrace his beloved and hold her in his arms, "*Abrazado con su esposa, que en sus brazos la traía, al cual la graciosa Madre en un pecebre ponía.*"[30]

These nine ballads provide a source for understanding the ecstatic and relational nature of God. They reveal a God who moves out in loving self-expression to make room for humanity. The way that Juan describes the interpersonal love that constitutes the mystery of God in Romance 1, "as beloved in the lover," parallels his description of the union between divine and human persons in "Dark Night" as "Lover transformed in the beloved."[31] As the *Romances* demonstrate, the Incarnation is the linchpin to understand the amatory perichoresis between divine and human persons. The Incarnation bridges divine and human life by opening the doors of the divine chamber.

The divine persons do not just make room for each other. The Incarnation shows that God makes room for us and all of creation. What interests Juan more than the intra-trinitarian perichoresis is the outpouring of divine love into human hearts. Therefore, it should not come as a surprise that sexual union provides such a fitting metaphor for understanding persons, divine and human, as ecstatic beings who make room for one another. Just as conjugal relations extend "the act of touching towards intensification," God's self-communicating love extends the triune life of God among us in a supreme act of hospitality. In this sense, "physically at least, there

---

[28] *Romances*, 7.

[29] *Romances*, 8.

[30] *Romances*, 9.

[31] See Colin Thompson, *St. John of the Cross: Songs in the Night* (Washington, DC: Catholic University of America, 2003), 57.

is no way to draw nearer to another than in sex, because in sex one makes room for another—quite physically, quite literally—within him- or herself."[32]

Juan discusses this life-giving and transforming divine act of hospitality as taking place primarily in the soul, "the dynamic and integrating spiritual reality that pervades human personhood."[33] But just as the itinerary of divine persons is not confined to the "inner" life of God (immanent Trinity), it is also not confined to the "inner" life of a person (soul).[34] Juan emphasizes that the lavish outpouring of divine love makes human persons full participants in divine life. This dynamic participation in divine life offers a new way of being and relating that impacts every aspect of human life, including, I would propose, human sexuality. I would also suggest that human sexuality can be regarded as an expression of the Spirit's activity in the flesh. It can be an experience that integrates the spirit and the senses, a sharing in the dynamism of divine love.[35]

---

[32] The last two quotes and the connection between sex and divine hospitality can be found in David Jensen, *God, Desire, and a Theology of Human Sexuality* (Louisville, KY: Westminster John Knox Press, 2013), 45.

[33] See Edward Howells, "The Dynamism and Unity of the Soul according to John of the Cross," in *John of the Cross and Teresa of Avila: Mystical Knowing and Selfhood* (New York: Crossroad, 2002), 40–59.

[34] See LaCugna, who cautions theologians about using phrases such as "immanent Trinity," "in God," "relations *ad intra*," the "inner life of God," "intradivine persons" as a way to distinguish "God as God" from "God for Us." Such use, according to LaCugna, leads theologians to construct the "immanent" Trinity as "God's interior state, God *in se*, and the economic Trinity to be how God is in the world, God *pro nobis* or *quoad nos*." The problem with this construction, she goes on to argue, is that "there is nothing 'in' God, as if God were something into which something else could be placed, whether it be attributes or relations or a trinity of persons." See *God for Us*, 224–225.

[35] See Howells's description of the way the soul in Juan's writings dynamically integrates spiritual and sensorial experiences in *John of the Cross and Teresa of Avila*, 40.

The Fluidity of Divine and Human Persons:
Personal and Dynamic

God is love, and human persons who are created in God's image participate in and embody this love. This Christian affirmation undergirds Juan's mystical theology, especially when he writes about the climactic and mystical moment of consummation between divine and human persons, which fittingly parallels the consummation of sexual union among human persons.[36] Mystical union is the summit of love that constitutes the most intense encounter with God. In his commentary on "Living Flame of Love," Juan speaks of it as an encounter with the Holy Spirit that divinizes the soul.[37] Parting the veil that separates divine and human life, the Spirit makes it possible to taste God's sweetness.[38]

---

[36] See also Juan's discussion relating the desire for mystical consummation to the beatific vision in Llama, 1.27.

[37] In Llama, 1.35: "Pero veamos ahora por qué también a este embestimiento interior del Espíritu le llama *encuentro* más que otro nombre alguno. Y es la razón porque sintiendo el alma en Dios infinita gana, como habemos dicho, de que se acabe la vida y que, como no ha llegado el tiempo de su perfección, no se hace, echa de ver que para consumarla y elevarla de la carne, hace él en ella estos embestimientos divinos y gloriosos a manera de encuentros, que, como son a fin de purificarla y sacarla de la carne, verdaderamente son encuentros con que siempre penetra, endiosando la sustancia del alma, haciéndola divina, en lo cual absorbe al alma sobre todo ser a ser de Dios. Y la causa es porque la encontró Dios y la traspasó en el Espíritu Santo vivamente, cuyas comunicaciones son impetuosas, cuando son afervoradas, como lo es este encuentro; al cual, porque en él el alma vivamente gusta de Dios, llama *dulce*; no porque otros muchos toques y encuentros que en este estado recibe dejen de ser dulces, sino por eminencia que tiene sobre todos los demás; porque le hace Dios, como habemos dicho, a fin de desatarla y glorificarla presto. De donde a ella le nacen alas para decir: *Rompe la tela*, etc." See also Javier Rico Aldave, "La Fonction Suréminente du Saint-Esprit selon 'La Vive Flamme D'amour' de S. Jean de la Croix," in *Jean de la Croix: Connaissance de l'homme et mystère de Dieu*, ed. Dominique Poirot (Paris: Cerf, 1993), 179–197.

[38] Llama, 1.35.

In his opening verse of "Living Flame of Love," Juan engages this erotic imagination.[39] He depicts the deep yearning that human persons have for the Holy Spirit as a desire to break open the veil" of the encounter between divine and human persons, "*rompe la tela de este dulce encuentro.*"[40] The suggestive sexual nature of this metaphor is verified in language of piercing and penetration found in Juan's own commentary on these verses from the poem.[41]

Such earthy language, I contend, invites us to ponder, rather than deny, the human barriers that keep us from loving and uniting

---

[39] Some scholars have argued that "Living Flame of Love" draws directly from the work of Garcilaso and Sebastían de Cordoba (as Juan himself acknowledges in Llama, Prologo, 4) in his use of such expression as "*llama de amor viva*" and "*rompe la tela.*" Others have also noted the connection to erotic and amorous literature of the time. Macpherson writes: "San Juan's dependence on the courtly tradition of secular love poetry, and on the *a lo divino* glosses which had become so popular in the late fifteenth and early sixteenth centuries, needs little further elaboration here: Dámaso Álonso is able to insist that with very few exceptions San Juan looked for his material either to the Song of Songs (for example, 'Cántico espiritual,' 'Noche oscura') or to the Peninsular tradition of profane love poetry (for example, 'Vivo sin vivir en mí,' 'El pastorcito,' 'Tras un amoroso lance'). By general consent, 'Llama de amor viva' falls into the second category." See Ian Macpherson, "Rompe la tela de este dulce encuentro: San Juan's 'Llama de amor viva' and the Courtly Context," in *Studies in Honor of Bruce W. Wardropper*, ed. Dian Fox, Harry Sieber, and Robert ter Horst (Newark, DE: Juan de la Cuesta, 1989), 195. Still, as Macpherson's observations evidence, he too falls into this unnecessary and false dichotomy between religious and profane literature, completely foreign to the popular imagination of Spanish culture and traditions—either preceding or concurrent with sixteenth-century Spain. I see little use trying to fall into this separation, as if one could separate religious and "secular" sources informing Juan's poetry and commentaries. Doing so fails to understand the religious mind-set at work in the Spanish mystic. Shari L. Lowin, *Arabic and Hebrew Love Poems in Al-Andalus* (New York: Routledge Taylor & Francis Group, 2014), 1 and note 1. For Juan's commentary of this expression *a lo divino,* see Llama, 1.29–36.

[40] "Llama," v.1. See also Llama, 1.27–29.

[41] Llama, 1.35; 2.9.

with one another. In this sense, we can affirm that the flame of love that realizes mystical union and constitutes human persons as God's beloved *is* the same flame of love that invites lovers to unite in nonexploitative and mutual sexual unions. This living flame of love consumes and consummates, thereby enabling persons to exist *for* and *from* one another as relational and amatory beings in God's triune image.[42] Juan uses the language of sexual arousal and climax to capture the human relationship to God that causes us to linger, in mystical union, in the arms of love.

Relationships affect all those involved. While Juan affirms Christian teaching on the immutability of God (*"Dios no se mueve"*),[43] it is unquestionable that "John of the Cross was influenced first and foremost by the personal, changing God of the Bible (who is hardly an unmoved mover!) and by his own meditative and contemplative experiences."[44] Juan's God is both active and passive, an agent of change with respect to us, but who also receives from us and thereby changes as a result of divine self-surrender.[45]

---

[42] I have previously pointed out that Juan wrote "Living Flame of Love," (a so-called "secular" love poem) while he was revising his commentary on "The Spiritual Canticle" (a so-called "religious" love poem). At the end of his commentary (CE, 39.14), Juan uses the metaphor of flame in connection with the Holy Spirit's consuming and consummating love. In doing so, Juan not only draws from biblical traditions, but clearly, he also had available other literary traditions common at the time. See Lowin, *Arabic and Hebrew Love Poems*, 7, 53, 153, 158; Dominique Poirot, "La feu, intime amour, dans l'enseignement de saint Jean de la Croix," *La Vie Spirituelle* 74 (1994): 613–625; Joaquín García Palacios, "Consideraciones sobre el símbolo de la 'llama' en San Juan de la Cruz," *La Espiritualidad Española del siglo XVI: aspectos literarios y linguisticos*, n. 501 (1990): 159–166.

[43] Llama, 3.11. See also S, III, 21; CE, 32.1.

[44] Daniel A. Dombrowski, *St. John of the Cross: An Appreciation* (Albany: State University of New York Press, 1992), 94.

[45] On the subject of "change" and divine kenosis see Walter Kasper, *The God of Jesus Christ*, trans. Matthew J. O'Connell (New York: Crossroad,

As Juan comments in his *The Spiritual Canticle*, "The power and the tenacity of love is great, for love captures and binds God Himself. Happy is the loving soul, since she possesses God for her prisoner, and *He is surrendered* to all her desires."[46] For Juan, God "changes" in the night that binds lover to beloved, without ceasing to be God. Why is this the case? Because that is the very nature of God's self-expressive love and relationship. God is disclosed in infinitely new ways as a result of relating and uniting with distinct human persons. LaCugna observes,

> With each new relationship we "are" in a new way, we "exist" in a new way, we have our being from an another. Since personal experience is constituted by relationship with others, we come to relationship to each new person in a fresh way, newly constituted by a new cluster of relationships, as a constantly new and evolving reality. We bring to each relationship our history of relationships, a history which is itself being created and expanded in every moment of existence. While the network of human personhood is limited, especially by its embodiment and its historical-cultural-linguistic conditions, to God belongs the sphere of infinite relatedness, infinite capacity for relationship, infinite actuality of relationship, both to past, present, and future reality.[47]

1989), 189–195 and Karl Rahner, *Foundations of Christian Faith*, trans. William V. Dych (New York: Crossroad, 1990), 215–227.

[46] CE, 32, 1. Emphasis mine. Cited and translated in Dombrowski, *St. John of the Cross*, 83. For a discussion on Juan's notion of God's immutability see ibid., 82–83.

[47] LaCugna, *God for Us*, 292–293.

Mystically Performative Fluidity

In his efforts to uphold the ineffability and mystery of God against all forms of idolatry, Juan uses divine names and divine attributes that can appear fluid in terms of gender and sexuality. In some ways this might be construed as anticipatory of contemporary feminist theological arguments that critique gender biases.[48] At times, his imagery challenges stereotypes that categorize the feminine as the passive and emotional versus the masculine which is associated with the active and rational.[49] While Juan does not escape socially constructed gender stereotypes, evident in his portrayal of the human soul as female spouse to a masculine God, he does portray God in both active and passive roles as a lover and as beloved. For example, in Romance 4 God is the Bridegroom who would take the Bride "tenderly in his arms / and there give her his love." In stanzas 6–8 of "Dark Night" God is the beloved, asleep on "mi pecho florido," the flowering chest of a human lover who caresses him and strokes his hair.

Such imagery today may be interpreted in ways that defy restrictive social constructions of sexual orientation and gender binaries. In the portrayal of the human soul as Bride and beloved spouse, Juan sees himself, and in this spousal imagery there can be a powerful resonance with human experiences of love in same-sex relationships. In his poetry, Juan performs his spousal identity with Christ in gender-fluid ways, sometimes as a woman and other times

---

48 See, for instance, Elizabeth Johnson, *She Who Is: The Mystery of God in Feminist Theological Discourse* (New York: Crossroad, 1992); Rosemary Radford Ruether, *Sexism and God-Talk: Toward a Feminist Theology* (Boston: Beacon Press, 1983); and Gail Ranshaw, *God beyond Gender* (Minneapolis: Fortress Press, 1995).

49 See Christopher Hinkle, "Love's Urgent Longings: St. John of the Cross," in *Queer Theology: Rethinking the Western Body*, ed. Gerard Loughlin (Malden, MA: Blackwell, 2007), 190, 192.

as a man.[50] As a woman, he expresses his "I" in connection to the soul in relationship to Christ, his bride, "*Amado con amada, amada en el Amado transformada.*"[51] Yet at other times this "I" also speaks in the first person, expressing his relationship to Christ as his male lover, "*¿Adonde te escondiste, Amado, y me dejaste congemido.*"[52] Willis Barnstone suggests that in "Dark Night," "Living Flame of Love," and "The Spiritual Canticle" Juan "speaks androgynously as a woman, as the anima, moving through darkness to light, in order to join her divine love in mystic-erotic union."[53] Commenting on "Living Flame of Love," he captures this fluid, and unquestionably erotic, nature of the mystical subject:

> We find a curious psychological duality here, for San Juan continues to speak as the woman and yet in the last line "the lover," *su querido*, is given in the narrative third person, meaning literally: "her lover." This is appropriate, for in this stanza of extreme eroticism, San Juan steps back, as it were, from the persona of the woman and seems to participate as both man and woman in the exploration. The fire image is continued, now as a lamp of

---

[50] On the notion of performativity see Judith Butler, *Gender Trouble: Feminism and the Subversion of Identity* (London: Routledge, 1990).

[51] For instance, see the poem "Noche," v. 5. See also "Cántico Espiritual," 12. On the use of the Song of Songs see Geneviève Fabry, "El Cantar de los Cantares en la obra de Luis de León, San Juan de la Cruz y Juan Gelman, Lengua, infancia y experiencia espiritual," *Teoliterária* 4, no. 8 (2014): 57–65; María González García, "Misticismo y erotismo: de San Juan de la Cruz a Pier Paolo Pasolini, Alegoría y teorema de la seducción," *Hispanic Journal* 33, no. 1 (2012): 49–60. Note that "*alma*" is gendered in feminine terms, even though it takes the masculine pronoun "el" (e.g., *el alma*) to avoid the awkward sound of la alma.

[52] "Cántico Espiritual," v. 1.

[53] Willis Barnstone, *The Poetics of Ecstasy: Varieties of Ekstasis from Sappho to Borges* (New York: Holmes & Meier, 1983), 171.

fire, a lamp to light up and fathom. It is the male image
of the penis examining "the lowest caverns of the sense,"
las profundas cavernas del sentido, where the caverns are
clearly the vagina.[54]

The central anthropological insight that Juan offers us is that to
be a person is to be an ecstatic being, in love, open to love, worthy
of love and through love that is transformative. Juan's deployment of conjugal love as metaphor for mystical union has positive
implications for considering sex and sexuality, whether that was
his intention or not. Juan's mystical performativity breaks from
traditional binary and essentialist constructions of the self. This
does not mean, however, that Juan manages to escape stereotypes
connected to gender, sexuality, and race in sixteenth-century Spain.
For instance, he takes issue with what he terms an "effeminate,"
afemidado, approach to religion and speaks in ways that many of us
would find offensive with respect to race and religion.[55] While Juan
embraces an integral anthropology, *"dos partes son un supuesto,"* and
while his mystical performativity invites consideration of gender
and sexual fluidity, as we understand from contemporary anthropological perspectives, there is no doubt that he remains a man of
his times, and as such, his writings at times reflect what we would

---

[54] Barnstone, *The Poetics of Ecstasy*, 186–187. Note that the poem
"The Living Flame of Love" portrays what could stereotypically be
conceived of as a male God who breaks the membrane of the sweet human
encounter, leaving an imprint on the breasts of the mystic in the ongoing
seductive playfulness of love. The possessive adjective used in this poem, *"su
querido,"* can connote either his darling, her darling, or its darling.

[55] For instance, in verse 24 of his poem "Cántico Espiritual," he begs
Christ not to reject him because of the dark color of his skin (*"No quiera
despreciarme, que, si color moreno en mí hallaste . . ."*). On the issue of
"effeminacy" see S, 3, 25. On the issue of religious/sexual bias see CE, 4.
On the issue of race see CE, 33, 3–9. See also Dombrowski, *St. John of the
Cross,* 99.

characterize today as sexist and heterosexist perspectives. Philosopher Daniel Dombrowski claims that while Juan does not avoid male bias, "he did a better job of avoiding male bias in religion than most systematic theologians and that contemporary individuals interested in gender issues in religion could learn a great deal from John of the Cross."[56]

Notwithstanding these limitations, Juan's mystical theology and his analogue of sexual union offer a disruptive way to speak about divine and human persons. The theology of this Christian mystic aligns with contemporary voices that critique essentialism and embrace more fluid and unstable approaches to divine and human persons. A mystic is a person who lives "identity without an essence."[57] Indeed, the mystic, who is the subject of Juan's writings, is like God, an ecstatic being. As dynamic processes, more than static essences, human persons become in the ebb and flow of ascetic life. Propelling this becoming is first and foremost God's desire for human persons. In God's living flame of love, this desire can be returned as human desire for God and expressed in the desire of human persons for one another.

On Divine and Human Desire

No discussion of Juan's theological anthropology would be complete without addressing the all-important category of desire within his theology. Sanjuanista scholars have pointed out that the category of desire is central to Juan's mystical theology: God's desire for human persons and the human desire for God and God's creatures.[58] Juan describes human persons as creatures of desire,

---

[56] Dombrowski, *St. John of the Cross*, 87.

[57] David Halperin, *Saint Foucault: Towards a Gay Hagiography* (New York: Oxford University Press, 1995), 61. Cited in Linn Marie Tonstad, *Queer Theology* (Eugene, OR: Cascade Books, 2018), 64.

[58] See Hinkle, "Love's Urgent Longings: St. John of the Cross,"

arguing that it is natural to be oriented to those things and persons that bring joy and pleasure to our hearts, even if these worldly objects of desire pale in comparison to desiring God.[59] This human desire for God is grounded upon and expresses the divine desire to unite with human persons. Christopher Hinkle observes that the writings of Juan unquestionably link gender transformation with the desire for God.[60] As mystics progress, they take on a more passive and receptive role, stereotypically associated with women. By the same token, Juan's God becomes increasingly more male. It is a God who Juan sees as penetrating the soul to rupture, *la tela*, the thin veil that keeps divine and human persons from mystically uniting.[61] Notwithstanding this gendering, what we find in Juan's writings is "not a constant gender performance but rather a desire-driven transformation toward an increasing receptivity and passivity before God."[62]

Although Juan's writings invite us to correlate sexual desire that leads to sexual union with the desire for God that leads to mystical union, these two forms of desire are not the same. Edward Howells offers an insightful analysis of the divine movement that

---

188–199; María del Sagrario Rollán, "Amour et désir chez saint Jean de la Croix," *Nouvelle Revue* 113/4 (1991): 498–515; Frank England, "An Architectonics of Desire: The Person on the Path to *Nada* in John of the Cross," *Acta Theologica*, 33, no. 1 (2013): 79–95; and Edward Howells, "From Human Desire to Divine Desire in John of the Cross," *Religious Studies* 55, no. 3 (2019): 405–417; Victoria B. Parco, "The Mystery of God and of the Human Person in San Juan de la Cruz," *Budhi* 5, no. 1 (2001): 37–51.

[59] "*Y cosa natural es que, cuando una cosa da gozo y contento al alma, si tiene otra que más estime y más gusto le dé, luego se acuerda de aquélla y asienta su gusto y gozo en ella.*" Juan argues that this delight for things of the world resembles God who even though God delights in all things does not delight so much in them than in Godself. See CE, 20–21,13.

[60] Hinkle, "Love's Urgent Longings," 191.

[61] Hinkle, "Love's Urgent Longings," 192.

[62] Hinkle, "Love's Urgent Longings," 191.

replaces the original incompatibility of divine and human desire with a graced relational mutuality that puts "continuity ahead of difference" between these two related but distinct forms of desire.[63] By drawing on the analogy of mutually shared love, Howells argues that Juan shifts the notion of desire from being solitary and unrequited, to one that is shared and reciprocal.[64] Understanding this move is essential. It helps to deepen our understanding of why sexual desire is such a fitting analogy for divine desire. Howells points out that the Incarnation enables us to understand the reconciliation of human and divine desire.[65] Moreover, it is Christ our beloved bridegroom who dwells within us and enables us "to move ecstatically towards God in an unlimited movement" that allows for finite desire to participate in divine desire.[66] Howells summarizes the trinitarian alignment of divine and human desire in the following way:

> John's understanding of the journey of human desire in relation to God is of a gradual transformation through a wide variety of manifestations of desire, which reaches a crisis, introducing a decisive change, linked to God's action in the incarnation, in which desire for God shifts from desire conceived as lack to desire as abundance. . . . John is

---

[63] "Through inclusion in divine desire, God is known not as an object outside the desire, but within it. . . . The continuity between divine and human becomes clear, and the difference is found as an internal distinction within this continuity, putting continuity ahead of difference." Howells, "From Human Desire to Divine Desire in John of the Cross," 413.

[64] Howells, "From Human Desire to Divine Desire," 415.

[65] Speaking of the soul, Howells writes: "John thinks that in her fallen state she has lost this knowledge of the continuity between human and divine desire, requiring the incarnation to make it known." Howells, "From Human Desire to Divine Desire," 411.

[66] Howells, "From Human Desire to Divine Desire," 412.

optimistic about the transformation of human desire into
the likeness of divine desire, taking on divine characteris-
tics. God can be known within the desire, in the manner
of the Father and Son in the Trinity, rather than as a quasi-
creaturely, external object; the same desire points to God's
presence in all human relations, making God available in
the world; and there is satisfaction in the continuation of
the desire without end, which detaches the pain of lack
from human growth.[67]

The desire of humans for one another, especially in sexual
desire, participates, reflects, and refracts divine desire. In Juan, as in
Teresa de Ávila and other mystics, human desire for God "encom-
passes the sensual and the sexual, so that they, too, might find their
continual source of delight."[68] Juan invites us to imagine that "God's
desire for us is *like* a lover's desire for the beloved, body, and soul: a
desire to touch, commune, be close, enter into, to make room for,
to taste."[69] This is why "Living Flame of Love," fittingly captures,
in the language of erotic desire, the human longing to linger with
and unite with God. Given the incorporation of human desire into
divine desire, it comes as no surprise that Juan speaks of human
persons tasting eternity using the language of lovers who delicately
and mutually touch and transform one another.

Speaking sanjuanistamente, we might say that "we desire as a
response to the God who desires us."[70] According to David Jensen,
mystics are highly attuned to the ordinary and to the flesh rather
than degrading the desires of the flesh and its expressions.[71] Mystics
do not call us to flee from the world.

---

[67] Howells, "From Human Desire to Divine Desire," 415–416.
[68] Jensen, *God, Desire and a Theology of Human Sexuality*, 31.
[69] Jensen, *God, Desire and a Theology of Human Sexuality*, 13.
[70] Jensen, *God, Desire and a Theology of Human Sexuality*, 29.
[71] Jensen, *God, Desire and a Theology of Human Sexuality*, 29.

One paradox of mysticism is this: the more intensely we are drawn toward our Beloved, the more fully we love the world. All true desire, according to the mystics, finds its home in God who loves the world. This homecoming in God, moreover, does not neglect our earthly loves; since our desire is always on the way to God, nothing is "left behind" as God cultivates desire in us.[72]

To think sanjuanistamente is to reject a dichotomy between sensuality and spirituality and to opt instead for an incarnational embrace of the ecstasy both offer. Hinkle cautions that some of Juan's writings, taken out of context, may seem to contradict this affirmation, suggesting instead "a fairly dismal view of sex," or that "all sexual desire must be eliminated in preparing the soul for God."[73] Keeping in mind Juan's concerns about idolatry and distraction helps to put in perspective what may appear to be anti-corporeal strains within Juan's theology of mystical union. Again Hinkle proves helpful: "The error here is not the queer claim that certain experiences of God have homoerotic content (or that certain homoerotic experiences have sacred content) but the privileging of the erotic as the sole, primary, or simply most appealing means for such experience and the concomitant tendency to equate unity with God with the satisfaction of one's own desire."[74]

To be human is to be a creature of desire.[75] "The human person, in San Juan de la Cruz's view, is a *mystery open to* Mystery, fully intelligible only from the perspective of the Mystery who is the Source and Object of the insatiable desire at the very heart of human existence."[76] Here Juan is reflecting Augustine's affirmation of

---

[72] Jensen, *God, Desire and a Theology of Human Sexuality*, 29.

[73] Hinkle, "Love's Urgent Longings," 195.

[74] Hinkle, "Love's Urgent Longings," 195.

[75] Rollán, "Amour et désir chez saint Jean de la Croix," 501.

[76] Parco, "The Mystery of God and of the Human Person in San Juan de la Cruz," 46.

the restless hearts that can find rest only in God.[77] The dark night
paradoxically increases the human longing for God, "*¿A dónde
te escondiste, amado, y me dejaste con gemido?*" (Where have you
hidden away, my beloved, and left me moaning?).[78]

The mystical journey can be described as a "purifying and
ecstatic itinerary of desire."[79] God offers Godself out of desire for
human persons in God's living flame of love. Desire drives humans
toward God and divine love itself steers the journey. *Ansia*, or the
yearning for God that persons experience, "*une séparation désider-
ante,*" characterizes each step of the way.[80] In "An Architectonics
of Desire," Frank England maps this itinerary of desire, which
requires not abandoning human desire, but rather disrupting all
unnecessary attachments so that every human desire, including
our sexual desires, can be reoriented to participate and reveal the
mystery of God.

> Therefore, finally, through following John's map, desire
> has been so attenuated to a residuum of unwilled persis-
> tence or to, what has been termed, "desireless desire." If
> such a reading of John's system may be entertained, then
> what John constructs appears to be less the ultimate nega-
> tion of desire than, instead, its reordering. Desire, as the
> very dynamic of being human and, moreover, as the very
> dynamic of the activity of a God, who goes out from its

---

[77] "Our hearts are restless until they rest in you." ["*cor nostrum inqui-
etum est donec requiescat in Te*"], St. Augustine, *Confessions*, Bk. 1.1.1.

[78] "*Cantico espiritual,*" v. 1.

[79] "*un parcours purificateur et extatique du desir,*" in Rollán, "Amour et
désir chez saint Jean de la Croix," 515.

[80] Rollán, "Amour et désir chez saint Jean de la Croix," 501, 504. Juan
uses "a constellation of terms" like *ansia* (yearning), *apetito* (appetite),
afición (orientation), and *pasión* (passion), all of them tied to the will, as
signposts that describe the dark journey of purification persons undertake
on their way to union with God.

own being in love—in the Son, and in the Son and the Spirit, and, indeed, to human beings in the passive nights in the desire of them—requires neither the destruction of desire or the desire not to map desire, nor the endeavour to render desire absent, but rather the incorporation of desire, and its admission as an enduring, if final posture of, presence in an architectonics of desire.[81]

The Spirit, as God's living flame of love inflames our *ansia*, our God-oriented human longing. This longing serves as a counterweight that offsets our disoriented appetites.[82] For queer persons it means rejecting what Hugo Córdova Quero describes as an oppressive colonialism, a "compulsive heterosexuality" that requires that "everything in society, from culture, fashion, the arts, film production, theology, sexuality and gender, be hetero-normalized."[83]

Mystical experience reveals the power of love and exalts the union with Jesus, the fusion between divine and human life.[84] It entails self-transcendence, but this human ecstasis toward God is a spiritual union that goes beyond the bodily even if at times it is experienced in the flesh. Mystical union makes our hearts beat faster, transporting our desire into the realm of the divine.[85]

---

[81] England, "An Architectonics of Desire," 93.

[82] "Voilà ce qu'est l'*ansia*: le contrepoids de l'appétit . . ." See Rollán, "Amour et désir chez saint Jean de la Croix," 508.

[83] Hugo Córdova Quero, "*Teo-queer-nautas: Teologías queer explorando nuevos horizontes en el siglo XXI*," in *Teorías queer y teologías: estar . . . en otro lugar*, ed. Genilma Boehler, Lars Bedurke, and Silvia Regina de Lilma Silva (San José, Costa Rica: Lara Segura & Asiados, 2013), 112.

[84] Coral Herrera Gómez, "La utopía emocional de la postmodernidad: el amor romántico desde una perspectiva queer," in *Teorías queer y teologías*, 53. Translation mine.

[85] "La experiencia mística revela el poder del amor y exalta la unión total con Jesús, la fusión de lo divino con lo humano. Es una unión espiritual que va más allá de lo carnal, si bien se experimenta carnalmente, porque

According to Juan, human persons can become divinized, transformed into God, full participants in the life of the triune God.
Because God has burned away the distance that separates Lover and
beloved, human persons can now be called living flames of love.

acelera el latido de su corazón, lo hace expandirse y encogerse, y transporta
a la conciencia a otras dimensiones." Gómez, "La utopía emocional de la
postmodernidad," 53.

5

QUEERING THE GOD DE AMOR

¡Cuán manso y amoroso
recuerdas en mi seno,
donde secretamente solo moras:
y en tu aspirar sabroso
de bien y gloria lleno
cuán delicadamente me enamoras![1]

Some scholars have characterized Juan's mysticism, and in particular, his commentary *Living Flame of Love*, as a practical commentary for Christian living, a pedagogical or, more specifically, mystagogical teaching intended to create new speech with respect to God and mystical experience of God.[2] While this commentary retrieves central elements of his mystical theology related to embracing the dark night, and the human process of purgation and illumination, its focus on mystical union and his deployment of sexual imagery tap into the more positive or cataphatic nature of his teaching. His use of sexual metaphors to

---

[1] "How gentle and loving my heart recalls, the place where you alone secretly dwell. And by your tasty breath replete with goodness and glory, how tenderly you seduce me!" See the poem "Llama," v. 4.

[2] See Gabriel Castro, "Llama de Amor Viva," in *Introducción a la lectura de San Juan de la Cruz*, ed. Agustín García Simón (Salamanca, ES: Junta de Castilla y León, 1991): 508–509.

deepen understanding of God's triune presence in our lives strate-
gically maps the journey to mystical union and paves new paths to
understanding the practical dimensions of his spirituality.

What might Juan's God-talk yield today in light of insights
from queer theologies? The turn to the bedroom and to expressions of love and of sexuality as *loci theologici* provide a point of
entry to consider a queering of our God-talk and its implications
not only for approaching divine mystery but for recognizing
the image of God embodied in LGBTQ+ people. As a mystic,
Juan de la Cruz deployed the language of romance, courtship,
and conjugal love as a means to understand and communicate
analogously the relationship and journey of the human soul to
divine mystery. Queer theologians today turn to the theo-poli-
tics of the bedroom and consider the much-neglected everyday
lives of people, especially the experience of subjects often erased
from history.[3] Marcella Althaus-Reid has argued, the "ones that
theology has classified and numbered as the Alien Nation of God
do theology in their bedrooms and can teach us a couple of things
about God, love and justice."[4]

---

[3] On God, sexuality, and queer theology see Marcella Althaus-Reid,
The Queer God (New York: Routledge, 2003); idem, "Queer I Stand:
Lifting the Skirts of God," in *The Sexual Theologian*, ed. Marcella Althaus-
Reid and Lisa Isherwood (New York: T&T Clark, 2004), 99–109; Linn
Marie Tonstad, *God and Difference: The Trinity, Sexuality, and the Trans-
formation of Finitude* (New York: Routledge, 2016); Sarah Coakley, *God,
Sexuality, and the Self* (Cambridge: Cambridge University Press, 2013);
Rolf R. Nolasco Jr., *God's Beloved Queer: Identity, Spirituality and Prac-
tice* (Eugene, OR: Wipf & Stock, 2019); Susannah Cornwall, "Stranger in
Our Midst: The Becoming of the Queer God in the Theology," in *Dancing
Theology in Fetish Boots*, ed. Lisa Isherwood and Mark D. Jordan (London:
SCM Press, 2010), 95–112; Gavin D'Costa, "Queer Trinity," in *Queer
Theology: Rethinking the Western Body*, ed. Gerard Loughlin (Malden, MA:
Blackwell, 2007), 269–280.

[4] Althaus-Reid, *The Queer God*, 36. For an excellent synthesis of her

I see Juan's mystical theology as disruptive and constructive. The apophatic elements of his theology guard against idolatrous interpretations of divine life and exclusive mediations of that life in human experiences. The constructive or cataphatic elements are particularly evident in "Living Flame" and its commentary. In this twofold process of disrupting and constructing, and in his deployment of sexual metaphors, I perceive an opportunity to offer a queer reading of his theology. To queer Juan is to engage in critical conversations that unveil forgotten or suppressed theological elements in his thought and open new horizons of interpretation that challenge heteronormative theologies of God. As Hugo Córdova Quero observes,

> Therefore, to queer the past is a performative disruption in order to open up spaces for other discourses from the past to arise and to be heard in the conversation nowadays, as well as dealing with the performances of different discourses in the academy. To queer the past is not to transplant gays, lesbians, bisexuals or transsexuals into the past, but to disrupt monolithic discourses that oppress historical periods. It also refers to the fact that we need to be conscious that our own lenses should be disrupted and that the result of that process of disruption is not to reiterate hegemonic heteropatriarchal discourses.[5]

I find in my reading of Juan permission to pursue a queer line of interpretation when he writes that "it is better to allow for a broad interpretation to these utterances of love, so that persons may

work see Thia Cooper, *Queer and Indecent: An Introduction to Marcella Althaus-Reid* (London: SCM Press, 2021).

[5] Martín Hugo Córdova Quero, "Friendship with Benefits: A Queer Reading of Aelred of Rievaulx and His Theology of Friendship," in *The Sexual Theologian*, 28.

derive benefit in accordance with the mode and capacity of their spirit."[6] As a Latino theologian, I am attracted to Juan's positive use of carnal language and loving imagery as a way of describing the soul's journey to and union with God. As a Latinx theologian growing into an understanding and lived experience of queerness, my own included, I am drawn more deeply into engagement with queer theologians and queer studies.

Situated at these intersections, I acknowledge that "different ways of amatory knowing express themselves in different ways of befriending, imagining God and compassion and creating different structures of relationships."[7] With that in mind, I now revisit my mapping of Juan's theology of God in terms of God-talk, God's self-communication, and divine and human ecstasis with an eye toward queering it in ways that enable us to know and name God as the queer God de amor. I queer Juan's God talk, exploring resonances between Juan's mystical theology and contemporary queer theology. I challenge the implicit and explicit heteronormativity of amatory conceptions of God's self-communication and turn to queer love as another expression and mediation of the self-communicative nature of divine love. I engage the ecstasis of divine and

---

[6] In CE, Prologo, 2; Note a similar argument in Llama when he writes: "and knowing the reader understands that everything I say is as far from the reality as is a painting from the living object represented, I shall declare what I know" (Llama, Prologo 1). Finally, note the following argument Celia Kourie makes: "John's entire mystical schemata must be seen holistically; the various stages may well overlap, and the path is unique to each individual: 'God leads each one along different paths so that hardly one spirit will be found like another in even half its procedure.'" Celia Kourie, "The Way of the Mystic: The Sanjuanist Stages of the Spiritual Path," *HTS Theological Studies* 72, no. 4 (2016): 10, http://www.scielo.org.za/scielo.php?script=sci_arttext&pid=S0259-94222016000400033.

[7] Lisa Isherwood and Marcella Althaus-Reid, "Introduction: Queering Theology Thinking Theology and Queer Theory," in *The Sexual Theologian*, 5.

human life in conversation with queer theology's embrace of sexual subjects and sexuality as dynamic. Finally any revisiting of an itinerary is an opportunity to note sites missed and alternate roads that may yield new directions.

Queering Juan's Mysticism, a Precedent

The allegorical eroticism in Juan's writings has already demonstrated its power to speak to LGBTQ+ authors, for example, in Spanish literature and in spirituality. The particular appeal of "The Dark Night" is worth noting. The sonnets of Federico García Lorca, a prominent Spanish literary voice, were inspired by Juan's love poetry.[8] García Lorca queers Juan in his *Sonnets of Dark Love*.[9] In García Lorca's poems, as is the case with some other Spanish writers, the phrase *"amor oscuro"* serves as a code for gay love. García Lorca borrows images from Juan like fire, darkness, hiddenness, wounded stag, and male divine lover, to name but a few. García Lorca's subject is undoubtedly the queer male encounter. Daniel Muñoz posits that "great love for the

---

[8] The sonnet (from the Italian *"sonetto"* or "little song" as a poetic form of fourteen lines. It originated in Sicily in the thirteenth century with Giacomo da Lentino and expressed courtly love. It was introduced into Spain in the early Spanish renaissance by Juan Boscán (1493–1542) and Garcilaso de la Vega (1501–1536). More specifically, its introduction in Spain can be traced to 1526 when Boscán met Andrea Navagero, the Venetian ambassador to Spain. Navagero introduced Boscán to the Italian sonnet. In turn, Boscán introduced it to his friend de la Vega who achieved its perfection in the Spanish language. See Willis Barnstone, ed. and trans., *Six Masters of the Spanish Sonnet* (Carbondale: Southern Illinois University Press, 1993), 1–4. Juan explicitly refers to Boscán as his primary source of inspiration for his poems. For Juan's attribution to Boscán, see the beginning of Llama, *"Canciones que hace el alma en la íntima unión en Dios,"* v. 4.

[9] See Federico García Lorca, *Sonetos del Amor Oscuro, Poemas de amor y erotismo, Inéditos de madurez*, ed. Javier Ruiz-Portella (Barcelona: Alterra, 1995).

sixteenth-century mystic and his poetry may partly be caused by
the way that John's homoerotic language resonated with his own
experience of love. That is, John of the Cross was able to express
some of Lorca's profound feelings and desires; desires that would
otherwise be silenced by society and even by the way he dealt with
his own sexuality."[10] Muñoz points out the influences of Juan in
García Lorca's sonnets.

> Most of these have one thing in common: they reflect a
> passion for life and a depth for love that both Lorca and
> John of the Cross shared across the time span. They also
> express love in very earthly and physical ways, even when
> the love described is of a spiritual nature. The earthiness
> of Spanish mysticism, compared with the more ethereal
> and philosophical central European and Eastern mystics,
> is well attested. This earthy spirituality is present in the
> works of the great Iberian mystics, from the writings of
> the Sufi ibn Arabi, to the Sephardic Jewish author of the
> "Zohar," Moses of Leon, to the Christian poems of Luis de
> Granada, John of the Cross, and Teresa of Avila.[11]

Indeed, both García Lorca and Juan reflect a long Iberian
tradition that drew inspiration from erotic poetry. The last
stronghold of Al-Andalus, Granada, the city where Juan wrote
"Living Flame of Love," and, over three centuries later, where
García Lorca wrote his sonnets, is heir to a legacy of homoerotic

---

[10] Daniel Muñoz, "The Spiritual Force of Unleashed Love: Echoes
of Saint John of the Cross in Federico García Lorca's Sonnets of the Dark
Love," *Spiritus; A Journal of Christian Spirituality* 18, no. 2 (2018): 166. On
the voice of the soul/author and the way it communicates Juan's mystical
experiences, see Castro, "Llama de Amor Viva," 503–509.

[11] Muñoz, "The Spiritual Force of Unleashed Love," 166–167.

love poems.[12] Louis Crompton, a pioneer scholar and professor in Gay and Lesbian Studies notes this erotic thread in Hispano-Arabic love poetry "by men to or about other males."[13] He continues, "In the literature of Sufi mysticism, rapturous poetry addressed to male lovers might even symbolize union with the divine. So Muslim religion paradoxically forbade, allowed, and exalted homoerotic desire. It provided striking similarities with Judaism and Christianity in the sphere of law but fostered a radically different literary, social, and affective atmosphere that was much more tolerant."[14] Some of Juan's writings have suffered the fate of the works of García Lorca, and other queer literary giants of the Iberian peninsula: the erasure of homoeroticism that has "taken place in three principal ways: misreading; the conscious use of ambiguity; and decontextualization."[15]

"To find St. John of the Cross teaching the due ordering of sexual to spiritual desire, and not the least for gay men," writes Gerard Loughlin, "is not to find John a gay saint, even if there are aspects of his life and character that tempt this identification."[16]

---

[12] See Shari L. Lowin, *Arabic and Hebrew Love Poems* (London: Routledge Taylor & Francis Group, 2014), esp. 47–83; Glenn W. Olsen, "The Sodomitic Lions of Granada," *Journal of the History of Sexuality* 13, no. 3 (2004): 1–25. As a result of heteronormativity and homophobia, homoerotic desire in the writings of Spanish literary giants of the past has been kept in the closet, abstracted and suppressed, even when the authors of these writings do not hide the gender of their desire. For instance, see Susana Cavallo, "Emotions Recollected through Antiquity: Francisco Brine's 'Poemas a D.K,'" *Hispania* 84, no. 2 (2001): 205–213.

[13] Louis Crompton, *Homosexuality and Civilization* (Cambridge, MA: Belknap Press of Harvard University Press, 2003), 167.

[14] Crompton, *Homosexuality and Civilization*, 172.

[15] Cavallo, "Emotions Recollected through Antiquity," 207. Cavallo makes this argument in reference to interpreters of the poet Francisco Brines Bañó.

[16] Gerard Loughlin, "What Is Queer? Theology after Identity," *Theology & Sexuality* 12, no. 2 (2008): 147.

Such characterization would be anachronistic. However, "we should attend to the queerness of his writings, to John's written desire for the embrace of his divine lover."[17] Within this context it is most appropriate to queer Juan's mystical theology of God, while not abandoning the specific sexual connotations in relation to LGBTQ+ communities. To frame Juan through the optics of queer theology means:

> In addition to the definition of "queer" as "odd", and as a collective grouping for non-normative identifications of gender/sexuality, there is a third, critical usage of the word which emerges from its use as an academic term. In this context "queer" means to "disturb" or "disrupt". It is this definition that was later applied to theory, and theology, as a critical lens. It calls for the uncovering and dismantling of power structures.[18]

Juan pushes our understanding of God beyond the merely cognitive and intellectual to embrace the language of affectivity and the sensual. His language may indeed seem disruptive with

---

17 Loughlin, "What Is Queer," 147.

18 Chris Greenough, *Queer Theologies: The Basics* (New York: Routledge, 2020), 4. On the term "queer" and its appropriations see Michael Hames-García, "Queer Theory Revisited," in *Gay Latino Studies: A Critical Reader*, ed. Michael Hames-García and Ernesto Javier Martínez (Durham, NC: Duke University Press, 2011), 19–45; Hugo Córdova Quero, *Sin Tabú: Religiones y diversidad sexual en América Latina* (Bogotá, Colombia: REDLAD, 2018), 62–77; Meg-John Barker and Julia Scheele, *Queer: A Graphic History* (London: Allen & Unwin, 2016); Linn Marie Tonstad, *Queer Theology* (Eugene, OR: Cascade Books, 2018), 1–15; Nolasco Jr., *God's Beloved Queer*, 13–32; Isherwood and Althaus-Reid, introduction to *The Sexual Theologian*, 1–15; Susannah Cornwall, *Controversies in Queer Theology* (London: SCM Press, 2011), 9–42; Loughlin, "What Is Queer," 143–52.

its affirmative use of erotic imagery to describe the relationship between humans and the divine. Juan's mystical theology of God may, in this sense, be considered queer. Unlike some queer voices in Spanish literature, few biblical scholars and theologians have attended to the sexual dimensions of Juan's writings, and rarely do they venture beyond the heteronormative sexual subject.[19] To some extent, Juan's own commentaries reflect this heteronormativity, but as we have seen, his poems also push and disrupt ways of conceiving the human relationship to God through his performance, for example, as Christ's mystical male lover.[20]

Queering God-talk Sanjuanistamente

Queer theology is less about sexual orientation and gender identity than it is about disrupting God-talk, although it certainly addresses these human experiences. Queer theology invites us to rethink where God can be encountered, how God can be understood, and how God can be named. It seeks to unmask gender and sex-based oppression. In this process of illumination and purification of our hearts and minds God can be set free from false ideological constructions that often originate in daily life experiences especially as they relate to the bedroom and in the privileging of heterosexism and gender binaries as normative.[21]

---

[19] Note that the most comprehensive Spanish bibliography to date on Juan de la Cruz only lists one entry in the subject index under the theme of sexuality. See "Índice analítico," in Manuel Diego Sánchez, *San Juan de la Cruz: bibliografía sistemática* (Madrid: Editorial de Espiritualidad, 2000), 726. For a heteronormative approach to the sexual analogues in his mysticism see Willis Barnstone, "Mystico-Erotic Love 'O Living Flame of Love,'" *Revista Hispánica Moderna* 37, no. 4 (1972–1973): 253–261.

[20] On the voice of the soul/author and the way it communicates Juan's mystical experiences see Castro, "Llama de Amor Viva," 503–509.

[21] Isherwood and Althaus-Reid, introduction to *The Sexual Theologian*, 5.

Surprisingly, contemporary queer theology may find resonances with Juan's mystical God-talk. Queer theologies and Juan's
sexual analogical imagery, each in their own way, make human sexuality a necessary part of God-talk. Juan embraces detachment as the
rule of self-discovery and self-actualization in God. This is Juan's
nada that leads to *todo*. Traveling down this path of negation calls
for the elimination of idols—all human experiences, concepts, and
practices that take the place of God. Queering theology, Althaus-
Reid explains, requires courage: "In the same way that people
sometimes need to renounce a beloved who has ill-treated them,
we face here the challenge of renouncing beloved sexual ideologies,
systems of belief that even if built upon injustice have become dear
to us, especially if associated with the will of God."[22] This purging
cannot take place without distancing ourselves from physically,
socially, and psychologically abusive contexts. For queer persons, it
requires courage to allow ourselves to be touched by God's flame of
love, to experience the dark night, and to denounce all that under-
mines our humanity. For Christian theologizing it means retrieving
Juan's sense of the integrity of body and soul in ways that empower
us to savor the divine presence in embodied sexualities.

In his reading of García Lorca through the lens of Juan's
poetry, Muñoz observes that "both poets meet on the ground
zero of unleashed love, where the wound of such love, necessary
or unavoidable, because it is true love, is felt in the flesh as much as
in the soul."[23] In that unleashed love that binds the two poets, he
perceives "a channel through which to express human desire and
longing with a profound spiritual force."[24] Muñoz's commentary
on Juan's imagery of resting on a lover's chest as a site of intimacy,

---

[22] Isherwood and Althaus-Reid, introduction to *The Sexual Theologian*, 3.

[23] Muñoz, "The Spiritual Force of Unleashed Love," 167.

[24] Muñoz, "The Spiritual Force of Unleashed Love," 167.

such that the heartbeat can be heard, helps expand our theological imaginations with respect to *loci theologici*.

> In "Spiritual Canticle," the bride describes the moment of deepest intimacy with the words: "there he gave me his chest" (stanza 27). Also in "Night," before the loved one reclined her face on the Beloved (stanza 8), John describes how the Beloved did a similar thing: "Upon my flowery chest, / which I kept solely for him alone, / there he fell asleep, / and I caressed him" (stanza 6).[25]

This appreciation for intimacy, which reflects both hetero-erotic and homoerotic manifestations, situates sensuality and sexuality as part of God-talk. Recognizing the "underlying homoerotic dimension" of Juan's God-talk, as Muñoz does, also opens the possibility for exploring how classical theologies already contain homoerotic imagery, to say the least.[26] Neglecting this aspect of God-talk reveals how deeply entrenched heterosexism is in Christian analogical imaginations to the point of ignoring or sanitizing its presence in the rich corpus of Christian mysticism.[27] Moreover, the failure in Christianity to recognize "different ways of amatory knowing" requires "questioning the love-talk of theology" and going "deeper into the structure of the Church, and the way that theology helps to present, support and understand the meaning of love in practice."[28] In other words, to take Juan's mystical approach seri-

---

[25] Muñoz, "The Spiritual Force of Unleashed Love," 160.

[26] See Willis Barnstone, *The Poetics of Ecstasy: Varieties of Ekstasis from Sappho to Borges* (New York: Holmes & Meier, 1983), 182–183.

[27] For an interpretation that relates mystical touch to homoerotic touch see Michael Bernard Kelly, *Christian Mysticism's Queer Flame: Spirituality in the Lives of Contemporary Gay Men* (New York: Routledge Taylor & Francis Group, 2019), 221–227.

[28] Isherwood and Althaus-Reid, introduction to *The Sexual Theologian*, 2. I borrow the expression "different ways of amatory knowing"

ously in light of the wisdom of queer theology means considering the bedroom, the embrace of a lover, and the experience of desire, as fitting sites to contemplate the mystery of the triune mystery of God, and in ways that are queer-friendly.

For queer persons entering the dark night might entail surrendering inherited myths of heteronormativity even if they are life-giving means of grace for straight persons.[29] Christopher Hinkle correlates this darkening of the spiritual faculties and senses with the feeling of abandonment that queer persons often experience. For queer persons embracing this "dark night," which he associates with social and religious oppressive constructs that unnaturally detour one's queer desire for God, is, paradoxically, the precondition for establishing the possibility of an intimate relationship with and knowledge of God.

> I do not suggest that all gays and lesbians are (or should understand themselves to be) involved in the passive purifications that John describes, but his description of an awareness of God's ongoing participation in one's life does offer a particularly apt model for making sense of gay religious experience. For those who pass through a period of feeling painfully alienated from God, such an awareness restores a sense of meaning and purpose. It also gives the experience of alienation, as well as its culminating insight, that God affirms rather than rejects same-gender love, an authority they have often been denied, providing an exit to the vicious epistemological circle within which the homosexual person's own inexplicable conviction of his rightness is taken as conclusive evidence of the influ-

---

from page 5 of that introduction.

[29] See Isherwood and Althaus-Reid, introduction to *The Sexual Theologian*, 4–5.

ence of sin and denial. John justifies the pain involved in this journey as necessary for the purgation of errors and miseries of the soul. Perhaps, then, those whose experience of God's affirmation of homosexual practice leads them painfully to abandon the creed or community in which they were raised are experiencing the necessary purgation of errors and miseries that accompanies increasing intimacy with God.[30]

By opting to purge theological errors—errors communicated through God-talk all too familiar within our families, our Church, and our society—queer persons challenge heteronormative and gender binary theologies that have themselves become idols and obstacles to ascending the mountain of love and coming to know the God who is beyond all names and experiences, the God that Juan knows as "*un no sé qué.*" The ascetic practice of unknowing in order to know is a necessary step for queer persons to experience and know God in their queer ways of loving and knowing.

> At the end of our hermeneutical praxis we are trying to unveil or re-discover the face of the Queer God who manifests Godself in our life of sexual, emotional and political relationships. This is a God who depends on our experiences of pleasure and despair in intimacy to manifest Godself, but who has been displaced, theologically speaking, by a God of grand heterosexual illusions, phantasmatic assumptions of the order of love and sexuality.[31]

The queer God of love "is not only non-habitual but also

---

[30] Christopher Hinkle, "A Delicate Knowledge: Epistemology, Homosexuality, and St. John of the Cross," *Modern Theology* 17, no. 4 (2001): 435.

[31] Althaus-Reid, *The Queer God*, 108.

omnisexual" in the sense that its triune mystery of love is lavishly shared with all and can be analogously conceived in more than just heteronormative love.[32] We need the humility to acknowledge that God cannot be confined to any closet, for God is indeed an "I know not what." In this sense, we will not be able to engage in queer God-talk "without understanding different sexual ways of knowing."[33]

Queering God's Self-Communication

Central to Juan's theology of grace is his understanding of God's nature as self-communicative love. Juan quotes the scholastic principle "Whatever is received into something is received according to the condition of the receiver" as an argument for understanding the reason for God's self-communication.[34] In our natural state, we are incapable of knowing and uniting with God. This is why God's presence is needed to transform human freedom. Under divine guidance, our willing and knowing become capable, first actively and then passively to receive God's triune life, which completes each person in accord with their particular ways of being human.

Juan presents us with metaphors to understand the triune life of grace, its self-communication, and its transformative effects in human persons. He leaves little doubt that his theology of God's self-communication operates *both* in the realm of the spiritual *and* in the body. God's love binds divine and human persons, transforming one into the other. It also binds human persons to one another.

---

[32] I borrow the expression "non-habitual and omnisexual" from Althaus-Reid. See *The Queer God*, 52–53.

[33] Althaus-Reid, *The Queer God*, 52.

[34] Llama, 3.34. See also N, 2.16.4. On the principle "*Quidquid recipitur ad modum recipientis recipitur*," see http://lonergan.org/2009/10/16/ applying-a-thomist-principle-quidquid-recipitur-ad-modum-recipientis-recipitur/.

Queering Juan's theology of grace is a necessary move in order to produce a more inclusive understanding of the varied embodied gendered and sexual ways that mediate the divine encounter with human recipients of God's self-communication. Critiques of heteronormativity and the exclusive use of heterosexual analogues to describe divine mediations of grace are not simply matters of academic theology. Heterosexism and heteronormativity impact our structures, systems, and relationships in ways that threaten the lives of queer persons, emotionally, physically, socially, and spiritually.[35]

Attitudes, systems, and structures that enable violence, exclusion, and inequality are contrary to an ordering of social relationships in accordance with God's relational and self-communicating love. For queer persons this entails embracing their particular and embodied ways of being sexually human. This acceptance affects spirituality, as Michael Kelly affirms: "If the mystical journey today is to be understood as fully incarnate, as the path of the entire embodied person and not simply that of a discarnate soul, then the sexuality and sexual awakenings of developing mystics must be taken seriously."[36]

---

[35] On the relationship between gender, sex, identity, and economy from the perspective of queer theologians see Althaus-Reid, "The Economy of God's Exchange Rate Mechanism," in *The Queer God*, 94–110, and Tonstad, "Money, Sex and God," in *Queer Theology*, 78–103. The disproportionately high rates of poverty, suicide, and homelessness among LGBTQ+ persons, especially LGBTQ+ youth remain concerns. In some countries today identifying as a member of the LGBTQ+ community and/or acting on homoerotic desires translates into imprisonment and even death. See ILGA 2019 world report on state sponsored homophobia, https://ilga.org/downloads/ILGA_State_Sponsored_Homophobia_2019_light.pdf. See also Miguel H. Díaz, "Remembering Stonewall: From Street Protests to Global Change," https://www.atlanticcouncil.org/blogs/new-atlanticist/remembering-stonewall-from-street-protests-to-global-change/.

[36] Kelly, *Christian Mysticism's Queer Flame*, 183. See also Michael Bernard Kelly, *Seduced by Grace: Contemporary Spirituality, Gay Experience and Christian Faith* (Melbourne: Clouds of Magellan, 2007), 4–21.

Scholarship that takes seriously the spirituality of contemporary gay men has taken great care in queering these encounters. In ways that parallel Juan's mystical journey of the active and passive night of the senses, Kelly describes the coming-out process as a risk-taking and grace-led journey.[37] He highlights the searing purification that queer persons often experience as a dark night that involves disinvesting from what they consider significant aspects of their lives, including seeing all concepts of God collapse.[38] For gay Christian men, Kelly proposes, the central question becomes how to reconcile the mystical and the erotic. This question, he affirms, is not just one among other theological questions to be raised, but rather, the most fundamental question to address "in the heart of this most central incarnational of religions."[39] It is a question that concerns God's life and its communication and expression *in* and *as* queer human life.

In "Living Flame of Love," Juan employs vocabulary that can also have erotic connotations like wounding, penetrating, touching, heating, caressing. Because many of Juan's interpreters read these metaphors through heteronormative optics, they apply them to God's transformative self-offer to human persons in terms of cisgender, preferably marital, imagery between a man and a woman. Reading Juan today through queer optics, I find there is an ambiguity in his analogous language that leaves open the possibility for fluidity in interpretation as well in his admission that "persons may derive benefit in accordance with the mode and capacity of their spirit."[40] Homoerotic imagery in relation to his own encounter with Christ, may resonate with the intimate experiences and spirituality of gay, trans, and bisexual men and the ways their love, in and out of bedrooms, participates in and reflects the mystery of divine and

---

[37] Kelly, *Christian Mysticism's Queer Flame*, 185.
[38] Ibid., 204.
[39] Ibid., 221.
[40] CE, Prologo, 2.

human communion. Juan's understanding of the soul is an embodied one, not one that bifurcates the bodily from the spiritual. His rich sensual metaphors defy sanitization, simplistic spiritualization, and narrow heteronormative interpretations. Muñoz captures this best in his commentary on "Living Flame of Love."

> In "Flame," the ambiguity and gender fluidity is even more puzzling. Whereas the male poet addresses the initial stanzas of the poem to a feminine gender "*llama de amor viva*" ("living flame of love"), in the last stanza the image changes radically. It is no longer an impersonal object ("a flame"), but a person ("the beloved"), that the poet appeals to. The mystic, this time without a female mask, declares to his male lover: "How gently and lovingly / you wake up on my chest, / where secretly you dwell alone; / and in your fragrant breathing, / full of goodness and glory, / how tenderly you make me fall in love!" The homoerotic echoes of this stanza, often overlooked by the critics, are consistent, nevertheless with John's broader poetic works.[41]

Of course, affirming this queer encounter does not exonerate Juan from the androcentric gender and sexual metaphors prevalent in his mystical theology. Queer women in particular, may find these metaphors deficient in their capacity to relate their experience of the divine with their sexual life experiences.[42] Juan's use of words

---

[41] Muñoz, "The Spiritual Force of Unleashed Love," 164.

[42] "The theological problem does not lie in reversion to naturalized sexual difference grounded in biology; the problem lies in the symbolics of sexual difference, which cannot be used to signify ontological difference without masculinizing God and rendering 'Him' an idol while rendering creation feminine in relation to 'Him.' Sexual difference cannot simply be reinvented theologically to get us beyond heterosexuality, for it is the

like penetration, in-dwelling, passivity, and activity to describe the Trinity and the process of mystical union privileges maleness, and today this limits its expressive power.

It is no surprise that Juan turns to human sexuality to describe the mystery of God and the life-giving relationship that ensues between divine and human persons. After all, human sexuality involves the capacity to give and receive life from others. In God's living flame of love, God unites with human persons, transforming one into the other. Like all persons, queer persons have access to this deifying and transformative power of the Holy Spirit that enables us to "know" God in ways that analogously resemble the sexual and embodied savoring of another, *"saber por amor."*[43] The Word becomes flesh so that the flesh can become Godlike. Therefore, as Juan would have us affirm, it is in the fortified and Spirit-enflamed flesh, and not out of it, that humans receive grace, consummate their love affair with God, and come to taste eternity.[44] Divine life overflows into human life in its incarnate manifestations of the life of God's Spirit, which of course includes, but is not limited to, sexual expression.[45] Reading Juan today through a lens attentive to his homoerotic imagery may signal a queer recognition in divine self-communication, a recognition that perceives sexuality as neither a burden nor a cross. Through such self-communication, "fleeting moments of queer recognition, of touch both human and divine, of communion and mystery can help us 'know how to live.' Recognition, like survival itself, is a gesture—fleeting, flirtatious, and

---

theological ordering of sexual difference that grounds and authorizes the hierarchical ordering of 'man' and 'woman' in the Christian imaginary." See Tonstad, *God and Difference*, 78. See also 220–246.

[43] On knowing as savoring, see CE, Prologo, 3.

[44] "Llama," v. 2; Llama, 2.21.

[45] Llama, 2.14, 2.22. See also Edward Howells, *John of the Cross and Teresa of Avila: Mystical Knowing and Selfhood* (New York: Crossroad, 2002), 35–36.

precarious—that stretches out her hand and says, Come."[46]

Queering the Ecstasis Divine and Human

In Juan's use of sensual imagery, the ecstasy of mystical union mirrors conjugal union that transports lovers beyond themselves. Queer sexual desire, Hinkle maintains, also "has been claimed by many as a critical point of access to God, an important clue as to what God may be, and John of the Cross both confirms and gives theological context for this experience."[47] The vivid description of sexual experience provided by one gay lover underscores the visceral power of Juan's analogies.

> You know, when you're hungry and you eat, your mouth feels good; if you want to hear beautiful music, it's nice in your ears; if you look at art, it's beautiful to the eyes. But there's something about sex, about the orgasm, that is every-where, you don't locate it, it overcomes you in a way that almost has no location ... there's also a brief respite from the incessant thinking mind. There's a certain acquiescence to it or submission, that your body just submits to, and there's something profoundly spiritual to me about submission in that way ... for that moment, it's like unifying all the parts of your body—it's not about the eye and the ear or the mouth anymore, it's about the wholeness of the body and just being overcome. There's unification in the ecstasy, and not just with you and the other person, but the very body that is you is brought together in this ecstasy, and I think there's something mystical about that.[48]

---

[46] Juana María Rodríguez, *Sexual Futures, Queer Gestures, and Other Latina Longings* (New York: New York University Press, 2014), 138.

[47] Hinkle, "Love's Urgent Longings," 188.

[48] Kelly, *Christian Mysticism's Queer Flame*, 153.

Hinkle cautions, however, that "theological accounts of sex should not ignore that sex also, where it is self-involved, shame-driven, or lacking in charity, can be a rejection of God, a point too often obscured for both straight and gay Christians by the church's single-minded focus on the gender of sexual partners."[49]

Muñoz reminds us that although Juan "experienced male friendships and intimacy in the context of convent community life with fellow friars, there is no evidence that he felt sexually attracted to other men. In any event, the love described by John, although charged with (homo) erotic imagery, always points beyond the physical to the spiritual, the sexual becoming a vehicle to channel spiritual longings of human-divine intimacy."[50] The elevation of the language of love and sexual attraction to describe mystical union in and of itself opens up a reconsideration and even a positive assessment of queer sexuality and sensual experiences as revelatory.

At the same time Juan's portrayal of courtship and erotic love is idyllic and utopian, disconnected in many ways from the realities of daily lives. Queer scholars of color insist that we must also challenge cultural, social, and economic structures that play an essential role in ordering human desires.[51] As Juana Rodríguez graphically reminds us, "Because we fuck against the walls of violence, the memory and threat of other forms of touch must forever serve as the constitutive outside to our utopian desires."[52]

Queering ecstasis means making room for those who have been rendered invisible, recognizing that the divine preferential option incarnated in Jesus's love for marginalized bodies includes "sexiled

---

[49] Hinkle, "Love's Urgent Longings," 188.

[50] Muñoz, "The Spiritual Force of Unleashed Love," 167.

[51] See C. Winter Han, *Racial Erotics and the Politics of Desire: Gay Men of Color, Sexual Racism, and the Politics of Desire* (Seattle: University of Washington Press, 2021).

[52] Rodríguez, *Sexual Futures*, 137.

bodies and their cultures."[53] Queer individuals and communities of color and their culturally embodied ways of relating to sexuality and the divine cannot be dismissed or subsumed into normative whiteness because both mystical and sexual unions are always experiences that relate to concrete and particular bodies. Making room for the forgotten other entails disrupting narratives that have failed to consider the intersectionality of sexuality, race, and culture. In this sense, queer theology itself cannot become idolatrous through neglect. Michael Hames-García challenges us to question issues of power and coloniality when it comes to sexuality.

> Are gay and lesbian identities simply complicit with the coloniality of power, or do they demonstrate a strategy of resistance to it, parallel to other strategies enacted by colonized and formerly colonized peoples? Is the question too complex for an either/or? And what are the possibilities for developing sexual identities that reject not only homophobia, but also the racism and Eurocentrism of the colonial/modern gender system?[54]

What emerges throughout Juan's poems that are under consideration in this study is a desire for an embodied intimacy with the divine, a mystical union that is captured in the language of human erotic love, a metaphor whose fluidity leaves open the sacramentality of queer love. In intimacy is found ecstasy; in ecstasy we

---

[53] I borrow this expression from Horacio N. Roque who uses it in reference to sexual migrants: sexiles are "those queer migrants leaving home/nation as a result of their sexuality." See Horacio N. Roque Ramírez, "Claiming Cultural Citizenship: Gay Latino (Im)Migrant Acts in San Francisco," in *Invisible No More: Understanding the Disenfranchisement of Latino Men and Boys*, ed. Pedro Noguera, Aída Hurtado, and Edward Fergus (New York: Routledge, 2012), 183.

[54] Hames-García, "Queer Theory Revisited," 42.

find God; and in God we find others in sexually and culturally embodied ways.[55]

A Journey toward the Queer God de Amor

As I was completing this book, I visited Sevilla, Córdoba, and Granada, in what was once Al-Andalus. I walked the grounds where Juan was inspired to compose some of his love poetry. In Granada, standing in this place where Juan wrote "*Llama de amor viva*," it was not hard for me to imagine the ways God's Spirit has come into my own life as a living flame of love. "Flesh carries memories of theological passions," writes Latina theologian Mayra Rivera.[56]

The God of Jesus Christ is a God of radical love who never ceases to go out to encounter us in our daily lives, *en lo cotidiano*. As a queer Latino, I have discovered in the outward and embodied expression of divine love, a God who, "in immoderate, intemperate, and scandalous loving ways,"[57] intermingles with our varied ways of being human. My own struggles reconciling my Catholic faith with my sexuality led me to explore Juan's writings, and in him I have discovered that the Incarnation is God's extravagant touch of humanity. Juan has helped me to understand that

---

[55] In her reflections titled "Sabor a Mí," Rodríguez writes: "Even in our most intimate moments, even our bodies seemed stripped of the material evidence of social worlds, the lingering taste of culture asserts force." In these reflections, I find resonances with Juan's epistemological affirmations of knowing as a savoring of divine and human life. See Rodríguez, *Sexual Futures*, 127.

[56] Mayra Rivera, *Poetics of the Flesh* (Durham, NC: Duke University Press, 2015), 1. See also idem, *The Touch of Transcendence: A Postcolonial Theology of God* (Louisville, KY: Westminster John Knox Press, 2007), esp. 83–97, 127–140.

[57] Elaine Padilla, *A Theology of Passion and Exuberance* (New York: Fordham University Press, 2015), 183. For a theology that explores divine enjoyment and in particular, embodied sexual love and desire see 86–120.

The realization of Negative Theology that G*d is beyond our epistemic reach, that He is neither male nor female, that She is neither not-male nor not-female, and the fundamental uncertainty on which all our knowledge rests is symbolized by and experienced through the queer body. This is the positive grace that we as queer men and women contribute to the Church; we are pointing to the fundamental reality of uncertainty and the troubling necessity of trust.[58]

Sadly, queer persons, myself included, have been socialized into thinking that our sexuality lies outside divine touch and thereby our acts of love that flow from our heart's desires rest outside the triune life of God. Juan's mysticism invites us to set aside confining notions of where and how God can be encountered. Juan's imagery invites us to tear away religious and cultural veils that keep us from knowing and loving a God who is boundless in love and omni-amorous with respect to all human persons and creatures. For Juan it is God who rests upon our flowering chests, and allows us to intimately savor the divine.

Too often our religious practices, spiritual traditions, and theologies have failed to offer queer persons resources for relating divine and queer life. Our Catholic imagination can appear limited and even alienating. I believe that Juan is one of those voices in our tradition that offers us language for resourcing our God-talk, rethinking our sexuality in affirmative ways, and recognizing ourselves as imago dei. Even if it is the case that God has remained hidden in our dark nights and in our experiences of *amor oscuro*, the human experience of this God is no less real and no less in need of

---

[58] Ludger Viefhues, S.J., "'On My Bed at Night I Sought Him Whom My Heart Loves': Reflections on Trust, Horror, G*D, and the Queer Body in Vowed Religious Life," *Modern Religious* 17, no. 4 (2001): 422.

theological articulation. Juan speaks powerfully to queer persons, for as he would have us imagine, God is discovered in hiddenness, because the Christian God is a Lover-God who sometimes hides in the dark of night. The question for us queer Catholics is not whether God has been present in our lives, but *where* God has been present in our queer and amatory experiences. *¿Adónde te escondite Amado, y me dejaste con gemido?*[59]

As Lover, God invites us into the divine chambers. As Beloved, God consummates and unites with us through Christ, our spouse. As living flame of love, God prepares and guides us to experience a life of ecstasis, a life that makes room for others, a life transformed. In our daily lives, we are each called to taste eternity in the healing presence of the Holy Spirit, the delicate touch of the Incarnate Word, and the gentle hand of the Creator: "*¡Oh cauterio suave! / ¡Oh regalada llaga! / ¡Oh mano blanda! ¡Oh toque delicado, / que a vida eterna sabe.*"[60]

---

[59] "Where have you hidden my beloved and left me moaning?" "Cántico Espiritual," v. 1.

[60] "¡Oh delicate cautery! Oh graced filled wound! Oh gentle hand! Oh delicate touch that tastes of eternal life and repays all my debt! By killing the old self in me, you turn my death into life." "Llama," v. 2.

CONCLUSION

What is not assumed is not saved.

—St. Gregory of Nazianzus

"The Christian's concern," as Walter Kasper observes, "is not with God in himself but with God-for-us, the God of Jesus Christ, who is a God of human beings (Heb. 11.16)."[1] Trinitarian theology is a theology of life which is birthed in love of God that includes all human persons. It is a theology that affirms how God shares Godself for our sake and for our salvation as Lover, Beloved Spouse, and Living Flame of Love. As human beings, we were created to exist in God's image and oriented in love to God and to our neighbors. Love, relationship, and community unite divine and human persons as well as human persons to one another. As Juan teaches us, love rightly embodied and expressed leads to union with God, and in God, enables other human amatory unions.

If Christ does not mediate the omnisexual mystery of God, and by mediating I mean a God inclusive of human experiences that can relate to persons on the basis of their gender identity and sexual orientation, then some members of the human family of God cannot be saved. This is a fundamental implication that we can draw from Christian soteriology. As Elizabeth Johnson writes with respect to women's embodiment, "If maleness is constitutive for the incarnation and redemption, female humanity is not

---

[1] Walter Kasper, *The God of Jesus Christ* (New York: Crossroad, 1989), 158.

117

assumed and therefore not saved."[2] Similarly, we can affirm that if heterosexuality is constitutive for the incarnation, if Christ and his offer of salvation can only be gracefully conceived through the experiences of a straight and male humanity, then queer humanity cannot be assumed, and therefore, cannot participate in God's triune and life-giving mystery.

Juan's mystical theology of the mystery of God presents us with a metaphysics of love. Divine love, Juan teaches us, is who God is. Divine love is what God wants us to be. But just like it is the case with God, so it is for humans: Love is not an abstract and static essence, but a communal, self-communicative, and interpersonal reality. Love, especially embodied and erotic love, is what queer folks are told they cannot gracefully give to and receive from others. Referring to the experience of a queer man, Michael Kelly describes his "profound impasse grounded in the deepest concern for life and faith."[3] "For David," Kelly affirms, "and perhaps for all Christian mystics in the contemporary world, a true dark night has to expose the deep, subtle, insidious rejection of sexuality and corporeality, of incarnation itself, a rejection that has masqueraded as 'purification.'"[4]

The question that many queer persons face daily in their lives is nothing less than the question of life. Queer persons learn at an early age that in order to survive, they must surrender part of who they are. In conscious and unconscious ways, our daily lives move in and out of the closet, as we discern, negotiate, conceal, and

---

[2] Elizabeth A. Johnson, "Redeeming the Name of Christ," in *Freeing Theology: The Essentials of Theology from Feminist Perspective* (New York: HarperCollins Publishers, 1993), 120.

[3] See Michael Bernard Kelly, *Christian Mysticism's Queer Flame: Spirituality in the Lives of Contemporary Gay Men* (New York: Routledge, 2019), 220.

[4] Kelly, *Christian Mysticism's Queer Flame*, 221.

reveal parts of our humanity within pervasive familial, religious, and social heteronormative structures. This often is an exhausting and life-draining experience. As a queer man in a Facebook post insightfully writes: "Queer people don't grow up as ourselves, we grow up playing a version of ourselves that sacrifices authenticity to minimize humiliation and prejudice." All too often, the cost of public self-disclosure is simply too high, as the loss of forty-nine lives at the Pulse night club in Orlando (2016) exemplifies.[5]

Reflecting on this tragedy, Xorje Olivares poignantly describes his reaction after Pulse, noting among other things, the interdependence of ethnic and sexual issues. Olivares recalls how not only the queer identity but also the Latinx identity of the victims was erased after the incident. Olivares discusses how Rudy, one of his Latinx friends, felt like a huge target had fallen on his back after Pulse. This experience only added to his already perceived religious persecution and his feelings of inferiority relative to white straight men. Rudy raises the following key question concerning his life: Why don't I feel safe being myself?

---

[5] For instance, see Roderick A. Ferguson, "The Pulse Nightclub and the State of Our World," *GLQ: A Journal of Lesbian and Gay Studies* 24, no. 1 (2018): 36–38; Elijah Adiv Edelman, "Why We Forget the Pulse Nightclub Murders: Bodies That (Never) Matter and a Call for Coalition Models of Queer and Trans Social Justice," *GLQ: A Journal of Lesbian and Gay Studies* 24, no. 1 (2018): 31–35. On the life-threatening consequences of being openly queer see Miguel H. Díaz, "Neighbors with Nowhere to Rest their Heads," https://www.ncronline.org/news/opinion/theology-en-la-plaza/neighbors-nowhere-rest-their-heads, and "HIV and Hispanics/Latinos," Centers for Disease Control and Prevention," March 18, 2021, https://www.cdc.gov/hiv/group/racialethnic/hispaniclatinos/index.html. See also the tragic story of Tyler Clementi's death in 2010 as a result of bullying, his parents' response in establishing the Tyler Clementi Foundation, and their fight to end faith-based bullying, which was part of the Christian upbringing of their son: https://tylerclementi.org/tylers-story-tcf/.

Olivares provides the following insightful response to Rudy's conundrum, highlighting some of the key forms of oppression that threaten the lives of queer Latino men:

> And it's a valid question, considering how tough it is growing up, and ultimately existing, as someone who is gay and brown. For instance, there's the weight of *machismo*, or overt masculinity, that dictates our early behaviors and mannerisms; there's the pressures of a religion, usually either Catholicism or Christianity, that shames you for your same-sex attractions; there's the lack of representation on *all* fronts that makes you feel worthless and invisible; and there's the persistent fetishization of Latinx people, particularly gay men, by those enchanted by our "exoticism."[6]

Issues of embodied oppressions, religion, and threats to life were not foreign experiences in Juan's own life.[7] During his nine months of solitary confinement in 1578, Juan suffered mental and physical abuse at the hands of religious men in his Carmelite community. While we have no way of knowing if and how Juan's own sexual experiences may have impacted his writings, we do know that a number of his theological perspectives came under suspicion by the Inquisition and were deemed to be heretical. In fact, he was linked to the *alumbrados*, a group that among other things came under suspicion by Church authorities for their views

---

[6] Xorje Olivares, "The Pulse Tragedy and the Ongoing Erasure of Queer Latin Culture," *Vice*, June 12, 2017, https://www.vice.com/en/article/ev45np/the-pulse-tragedy-and-the-ongoing-erasure-of-queer-latin-culture.

[7] For a discussion on the distinction between perfection and salvation in Juan's writings and on the degrees of union, see E. W. Trueman Dicken, *The Crucible of Love: A Study of the Mysticism of St. Teresa of Jesus and St. John of the Cross* (New York: Sheed and Ward, 1963), 463, 490.

of sexuality, including homosexuality.[8] We can also consider the case of Marina de San Miguel in colonialized America. Marina was a Dominican beata born around 1544, who despite her reputation as "a woman of great devotion," came to the attention of the Inquisition for her views of sexuality.[9] Like Juan, she was accused of being an *alumbrada*.[10] In Marina's case, however, she was tried as a sexual criminal for succumbing to the devil's heteroerotic *and* homoerotic seductions. She was publicly humiliated and forced to recant for her sins.[11] Her hesitation to confess the "sinful" nature of her sexual acts, which included self-pleasure and fantasizing sexual relations with both men and women, was used as evidence of her *alumbradismo*.

---

[8] On the history and theology of *alumbrados* and their understanding of sexual sins see Melquiades Andres, *La teología Española en el siglo XVI*, vol. II (Madrid: Biblioteca de Autores Cristianos, 1977), esp. 243–252. The Augustinian Basilio Ponce de León, professor of theology at Salamanca and nephew of Luis de León, strongly defended John's orthodoxy. Bernard McGinn, *Mysticism in the Golden Age of Spain*, vol. 6, part 2 of *The Presence of God: A History of Western Christian Mysticism* (New York: Crossroad, 2017), 238. On Luis de León's defense of Juan see "Reply of R.P.M. Fray Basilico Ponce de León, Prima Professor of Theology in the University of Salamanca, to the Notes and Objections which were Made Concerning Certain Propositions taken from the book of our Father Fray John of the Cross" (July 11, 1622), in *The Complete Works of Saint John of the Cross*, trans. E. Allison Peers; ed. P. Silverio de Santa Teresa (Westminster, MD: Newman Press, 1964), 382–434.

[9] See Jacqueline Holler, "'More Sins Than the Queen of England': Marina de San Miguel before the Mexican Inquisition," in *Women in the Inquisition: Spain and the New World*, ed. Mary E. Giles (Baltimore: Johns Hopkins University Press, 1999), 209–228; Jacqueline Holler, "The Spiritual and Physical Ecstasies of a Sixteenth-Century Beata: Marina de San Miguel Confesses before the Mexican Inquisition," in *Colonial Lives: Documents on Latin American History*, 1550–1850, ed. Richard Boyer and Geoffrey Spurling (New York: Oxford University Press, 2000), 79–98.

[10] Holler, "More Sins Than the Queen of England," 222.

[11] Holler, "More Sins Than the Queen of England," 223–227.

To state the obvious, the past and the present reveal to us that our notions of human sexuality, and how we use those notions to construct our theologies of God, contribute to much unnecessary human suffering. Perhaps Billy Porter, a popular contemporary icon in the lives of queer persons, puts it best when he observes, "The first thing that's taken away from us as LGBTQ people, from everybody, is our spirituality, is God."[12] This book paves an alternative and disruptive cartography. It maps the presence of the triune mystery God in queer lives. In line with the central teaching of Christian faith, namely the Incarnation, I invite the reader to consider the possibility of seeing the embodied spiritualities of queer persons and their sexual expressions as life-giving acts of self-expressive love, as vestiges of the Trinity. Thus, rather than stripping God from queer experiences, as Porter regrettably laments, what needs to be done is to fully locate the mystery of God in these experiences. A religious tradition like the Catholic tradition, which deeply values the relationship between faith and reason, can no longer ignore the experiences of LGBTQ+ persons of faith, their spiritualities, and the growing body of scholarship in the area of queer theology. Doing theology sanjuanistamente opens pathways for expanding and exploring Catholic interpretations in these areas.

Theology needs to begin, *en lo cotidiano,* in the minds and hearts and prayers and lives of concrete human beings.[13] A theology that fails to take into account the lived experiences, the sexuality, and spiritualties of queer persons cannot claim to be "catholic." Surely, we cannot reduce humanity to sexuality, nor should we ever equate salvation with sex. That said, neither should we dismiss

---

[12] Patrick Kelleher, "Billy Porter Hits Back at Christian Homophobes after Coming Out as HIV Positive: 'God doesn't hate f*gs,'" *Pink News,* May 20, 2021, https://www.pinknews.co.uk/2021/05/20/billy-porter-hiv-diagnosis-tamron-hall-pose/.

[13] See M. Shawn Copeland, *Desire, Darkness, and Hope: Theology in a Time of Impasse* (Collegeville, MN: Liturgical Press, 2021), 50.

outright sexuality and sexual union, nor, more specifically, queer
sexuality and queer sexual unions, as lying outside the salvific will
of God. Such claims limit the omnisexual and life-giving presence
of God in history. In Chalcedonian fashion, we must distinguish,
but never separate, the trinitarian life of God from the human
experiences of sexuality.[14]

We must overcome our theological timidity to address issues of
God and sexuality, especially those of us who passionately care for
issues of justice, equality, and the liberation of all persons. Our failure
to do so in the past evidences that when it comes to soteriology, our
"catholicity" has not been fully inclusive of all persons and issues of
life.[15] But since salvation depends upon God, and not on the omissions of our God-talk, our theological task is to catch up to the queer
experiences where God can be found, because God finds us in queer
sexuality and sex, "just like God finds us wherever we are."[16] Indeed,
God can be savored, wherever daily life is proclaimed:

As difficult as this queer brown life can be sometimes,
especially post-Pulse, it's mine—it's *ours*. We have the privilege to enjoy it, and I, personally, am more determined

---

[14] See Gustavo Gutiérrez, *The Truth Shall Make You Free*, Confronta-
tions (Maryknoll, NY: Orbis Books, 1990), 121–124.

[15] In constructing this argument, I am indebted to Orlando O. Espín,
Grace and Humanness: Theological Reflections Because of Culture (Mary-
knoll, NY: Orbis Books, 2007), 57. As an example of a Latinx approach to
soteriology that fails to address the oppression of queer persons as an issue
of communal life, survival, and salvation see Miguel H. Díaz, "Outside the
Survival of Community There Is No Salvation: A U.S. Hispanic Catholic
Contribution to Soteriology," in Orlando O. Espín, *Building Bridges, Doing
Justice: Constructing a Latino/a Ecumenical Theology* (Maryknoll, N.Y.:
Orbis Books, 2009), 91–111; Nancy Pineda Madrid, *Suffering and Salva-
tion in Ciudad Juárez* (Minneapolis: Fortress Press, 2011).

[16] David Jensen, *God, Desire, and a Theology of Human Sexuality*
(Louisville, KY: Westminster John Knox Press, 2013), 37.

than ever before to do just that. Not everyone receives that blessing, and I don't take my fortune lightly; not when 49 people were senselessly deprived of their own. So in the words of the Queen of Salsa, Celia Cruz, in her iconic *Carnaval* hit, we must know that *"la vida es una hermosura, hay que vivirla"* —life is beautiful, we must live it.[17]

"If someone is gay and he searches for the Lord and has good will, who am I to judge?" These are the powerful and life-giving words that Pope Francis uttered in 2013, which offered a glimmer of hope to queer persons, and in particular queer Catholics all over the world. This book's rethinking of the mystery of God sanjuanistamente considers queer persons, our sexuality, and our sexual unions to be part of the universal salvific will of God. As queer persons, we are intrinsic and indispensable members of the catholicity of the body of Christ, a crucified and risen "body" in whom the binaries of maleness and femaleness, heterosexuality and homosexuality, cis and trans, have all been overcome (Gal. 3:28).

---

[17] Olivares, "The Pulse Tragedy and the Ongoing Erasure of Queer Latin Culture." On-line citation above. On soteriological implications of the songs of Celia Cruz, see Díaz, "Outside the Survival of Community There Is No Salvation," 105–106.

INDEX

Academy of Catholic Hispanic
  Theologians of the United
  States (ACHTUS), xx
Al-Andalus, tradition of love
  poems in, xxi–xxii, 25, 98,
  114
alienation, 104, 115
Althaus-Reid, Marcella
  God-talk, rethinking from the
    bedroom, 24, 94
  on irruption of the sexual
    subject in history, 18, 29–30
  queering theology, on the
    courage needed for, 102
alumbrados group, 120–21
amor oscuro experience, 97, 115
analogical imagination, xxv, 26,
  103
ansia (yearning), 90–91
apophatic way
  on the dark night of knowing,
    34–38
  false attachments, avoiding, 40
  idolatrous interpretations of
    divine life, guarding against,
    95
  light as bridging the apophatic
    and cataphatic ways, 47
  negation of the senses and, 61
Aquinas, Thomas, 30–32, 74
"An Architectonics of Desire"
  (England), 90–91

Athanasius of Alexandria, 75
Augustine of Hippo, 31, 73,
  89–90

Barnstone, Willis
  on the androgynous tone of
    Juan de la Cruz, 83
  Cruz love poetry, on Spanish-
    world commentary, 24
  "The Dark Night," on
    directness in, 26
  "Living Flame of Love"
    commentary, 42
  on synesthetic significance of
    saber, 41
Burrows, Ruth, 35, 43

"Cántico Espiritual" (poem), xxi
cataphatic way, 34, 47
  cataphatic way of knowing
    God, 38–43
  Juan de la Cruz as a cataphatic
    theologian, 61
  in *Living Flame of Love,* 93, 95
Copeland, Shawn, 7
Córdova Quero, Hugo, 91, 95
lo cotidiano (daily living), 114,
  122
  describing and defining, 6–7
  queer reflection on, 18
  in theology done latinamente,
    2, 19

125

"The Living Flame of Love" (poem)
(continued)
Living Flame of Love
commentary, 20, 63–65, 78
as a practical commentary for
Christian living, 93
self-communicating love of
God, highlighting, 70–71
sexual love, using language of,
41–42
Trinitarian mystery of God,
understanding via, 46
widowed woman, asking for
commentary on, 27
locus theologicus
lo cotidiano, functioning as, 6–7
sexuality, placing in, 16, 26, 94,
102
Loughlin, Gerard, 28–29, 99
Lowin, Shari, xxii

Maximus the Confessor, 71
Mercado Y Peñalosa, Ana, xxiii
Muñoz, Daniel
on homoerotic dimension of
Juan's God-talk, 97–98, 103
human-divine intimacy, on
channeling longing for, 112
"Living Flame of Love,"
commentary, 109
loci theologici, expanding
possibilities for, 102
mysticism
as infused contemplation, 36
mystically performative fluidity,
82–85
poetry, as expressed through,
11–15, 16, 26, 54
popular Catholicism and,
9–11

queering of mystical Trinitarian
thought, 18–19
relevance of mystical theology,
48
as savoring of the divine
beloved, 1–2
sexuality and mysticism, 7–9,
17, 22–23
Sufi mystics, 98, 99
See also apophatic way;
cataphatic way; self-
communication of God;
triune mystery of God

Nanko-Fernández, Carmen,
6–7, 19–20
negative theology, 114–15
Nickoloff, James B., 17

Observants, order of, 4
Olivares, Xorje, 119–20
O'Meara, Thomas F., 2
On the Trinity (Augustine), 73
option for culture, x, xx, 19
option for the bedroom, 23–30

perichoresis (triune relations),
71–72, 75, 76
popular Catholicism, 9–11
Porter, Billy, 122
Pseudo-Cyril, 71

Rahner, Karl, 57
mysticism, use of term, 22
poetic word, on the primordial
function of, 13–14
spiritual-personal beings, on
humans as, 52–53
Trinity in Rahnerian terms, 54
Richard of St. Victor, 73

CPSIA information can be obtained
at www.ICGtesting.com
Printed in the USA
LVHW111105090822
725449LV00013B/376

9 781531 502478